Celebrate

With The Jewish Princess

Matzos!

Celebrate with the jewish princess

Recipes to make fantastic feasts and festivals for family and friends

Georgie Tarn & Tracey Fine

quadrille

This paperback edition first published in 2010 by
Quadrille Publishing Limited
Alhambra House
27-31 Charing Cross Road
London WC2H 0LS

Editorial director Jane O'Shea
Project editor Jamie Ambrose
Senior Designer Claire Peters
Designer Ros Holder
Illustrator Karen Greenberg
Production Director Vincent Smith
Production Controller Denise Stone

Cataloguing in Publication Data: a catalogue record for this book is available from the British Library.

ISBN-13 978 184400 832 2

Printed and bound in Singapore

dedication

We dedicate this book to our Queen Mothers, who, like a great pair of jeans, keep getting better with age. (Who do you think taught us the meaning of 'self-maintenance'?) They always give us advice, whether asked for or not. ('I don't want to interfere, but...') They are always at the end of the phone – wherever they happen to be! They go out of their way to make sure we have everything they never had – and give us everything they don't want. They know every ailment. Either they have heard of it, know someone who has had it, or they've had it themselves. They know every specialist for every ailment and make regular royal appointments.

We know you are very proud of us, because you tell the whole world. Keep it up: it's fabulous PR! Put this in your *naches* book!

contents

acknowledgements

Well, we've done it. WE ARE AUTHORS! *The Jewish Princess Cookbook* is in print. It's extraordinary that, for Princesses who love new products (especially anti-wrinkle creams; we always live in hope of finding one that WORKS), we have created a product ourselves! We can go shopping for our own creation.

Not that we *do*...

Well, OK. So there are just a few copies hidden under the bed.

Yes, being stacked on shelves has become a shopping kick. We enter a bookshop and our pulses begin to race. We see *The Jewish Princess Cookbook* and our hearts start to pound. We hide behind bookcases to see if there are any Princess Punters. When they appear (we're prepared to wait *hours*), our pink pens are ready to sign.

WE ARE OUR OWN STALKERS!

To be honest, this whole book thing came as a bit of a shock to our Princess Pals. They simply couldn't believe we had written a book. After all, whenever we mentioned the word 'book', they immediately started suggesting restaurants. (Nowadays, of course, we are 'booked' at all the trendiest fusions.) So we gave up and decided to keep it a secret.

Actually, we really enjoyed leading a Princess double life. If we were caught in town in Princess Power-suits (retro-*Dynasty*), we said, 'Consultation,' and our Princess Pals gave us that knowing look. When spotted buying copious amounts of food, we said, 'Family.' They looked sympathetic. When we had to fly to New York, yes, you guessed it: we said, 'SHOPPING!'

We were immediately given a list.

Now they all know the big secret. We broke the news at a dinner party (you should have seen their faces). After the initial 'WHY DIDN'T YOU TELL US?', they were all ultra-enthusiastic and began to nag us to get back on our thrones (well, we *are* JPs) and start typing *a new one*.

So as we sat there, wondering whether we could do it again. Would we Princess Panic: be thrown into early literary menopause and need CF – Calves Foot Jelly (a kosher savoury delicacy) – to get our creative juices flowing? NEVER! We just remembered to be PPP:

*POSITIVE,
*PRODUCTIVE,
*And, of course, PRINCESSLIKE!

So here we are: again!

To reach the summit of success (first or second time) you need a lot of help. We have to say that our friends, family, colleagues and even complete strangers (the couple on the airplane to Spain; you know who you are) came up trumps.

So a great big Honey Cake Hug to the following: our mothers, Helen Fine and Sandra Chester, for interior-designing bookstores globally, moving *The Jewish Princess Cookbook* to prime position; our fathers, Tony Fine and David Chester, still on the golf course (their handicaps haven't improved); in-laws Bobbie and Irvin Tarn, for cross-Atlantic advice (they have flown the coop to sunny Florida); and Birgitta Simone, Hayley Leslie, Lisa Tray, Vanessa Class and Michelle Grossman, for doing the school-run when Princesses G & T are out on Princess Meetings.

Many thanks, too, to the following Princesses for their input: Louise Caplin, Katie Vincent, Sima Fine, Zilda Collins, Lynda Brown, Sonia Levy, Monica Slater, Gillian Marsden, Elaine Grant, Karen Tarn, Cindy Kariel, Karen Gerrard, Mandy Stanley, Roz Laren, Louise Harris, Joanne Kaye, Deborah Bright, Debbie Addler, Lisa Marks, Mandy and Amanda Chester and Auntie Rosalind Chester.

And thank you to Rabbi Meir Salasnik for answering the Rabbi hotline with help and advice. Also to Victor Kramer (kosher texter); Andrew Thompson, our lawyer, who keeps getting us out of sticky situations; Tony and Richard from ABDA, our website designers: thank you, thank you!

Catherine in Harrods, who told us our book would be *huge*; Carolynne Wyper: a GEM! Then there's Anne-Marie, The Hairdresser, who drops everything for a JP crisis; Adam Lawrence, Royal Photographer; Dorie, our literary agent, who we still drive insane 24/7 and has become a great friend; Anne Kibel, our management agent (who we will drive mad): welcome aboard; Nick Painter, Waitrose Wonderman; Karen Greenberg, our illustrator: a Princess in The Big Apple; Claire Peters, JP Stylist; Mark McGinlay, our PR Prince at Quadrille; David Segrue: we will sign for you any time, any place, anywhere; Jane O'Shea and all at Quadrille who make dreams come true; Jamie Ambrose, our lovely, understanding editor: hope we didn't give you too much work this time round!

And of course, our brothers, sisters, sisters-in-law, nieces and nephews for tasting all our teatime treats; Caroline Sammuels: whenever we meet, you offer a pearl of wisdom; Stephen Marks, for trying to explain VAT (Very Aggravating Tax!): we still don't get it; our children, Max, Channie, Cassie, Eden and Darcy: culinary critics; Rat, Georgie's Prince Charming: thank you for all your time, support (this isn't just financial!) and belief in The Jewish Princess project (he's hoping to retire...).

And finally, thank you to all our Princess fans from all over the world. We love you dearly and are sure you will see us hiding in your bookstore soon, pink pens at the ready.

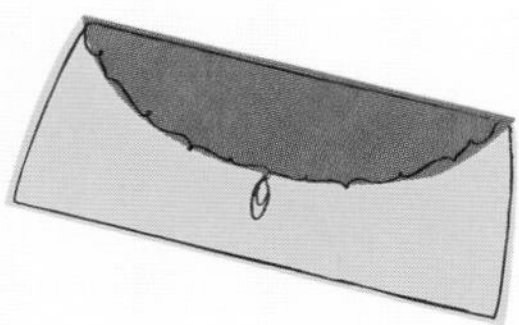

What does a Jewish Princess write?

Cheques!

Matzos!
Matzos!

mazel tov & siman tov

celebrate good times – come on!

I am now officially over my midlife crisis, but don't worry: I haven't had THE face-lift – *yet*. (It's amazing what a fabulous new haircut can do...) I have, however, come to an age when it's time to take stock, and this doesn't just mean chicken soup.

When I left my mother's womb – by Caesarean, of course – the first words I heard were *Mazel Tov*. I was bundled up, washed, weighed (the first of many times), fingers and toes counted, and then put into my very first new OUTFIT (again, the first of many!). *Lechayim* chimed around the room; the blessing means 'To life', and was bestowed upon me so that I would *live*, therefore it was my Princess duty to carry this out to the FULL.

Unlike Forrest Gump, my life is *not* like a box of chocolates – even though I do, of course, have a special Princess Passion for chocolate. My life is a buffet: a metaphorical table that stretches out before me, crammed full with a cornucopia of flavours and experiences. There are so many choices that it's difficult to Princess Pick, but my advice is to try a *bissel* of everything. If there's a queue, you might even be inclined to push forward, but if you do, then you might also miss out on meeting that special person standing right by your side. However, when you reach the end of the buffet, are full to the brim and cannot take another bite, the most important thing is that you'll know you have lived, loved and ENJOYED.

So, speaking of enjoyment, there's no time to waste: grab your Princess Plate, knives, forks, handbags – and shoes, of course. You are invited to join the queue at my buffet, to whine and dine at my table, to share my festivals and feasts with family and friends, and to hear some pearls of wisdom and gain some diamond advice along the way. Of course, you're also invited to try my delicious, new and easy recipes for all these special occasions.

Yes, The Jewish Princess is back, with her hair and nails done, so it's time once again to INDULGE!

let me present...

Like all Princesses I love making a *shiddach* (a successful introduction), so here goes:

DO I HAVE SOME RECIPES FOR YOU!

There are certain foods you are introduced to in your life which have such a profound effect on you that, whenever you eat them, see them or even sniff them, you are transported back to a time where you either bonded forever or were confounded that people could touch the stuff (a bit like blind dates).

I have to say that, with most dishes, one taste and I was hooked. However, a few foods still do produce Food Fear. It is odd, because as a child experiencing Jewish cuisine, I did eat some rather strange things. The chicken's foot, for example: you cannot find a stranger food, yet after it has been boiled in soup, sucking on such a foot (belonging only to a chicken, mind you) was and is an absolutely delicious experience, as was eating liver and even oxtail. Now, even though a chicken's foot definitely *looks* like a chicken's foot, I never had a problem with it, yet if you so much as mention TONGUE, I feel the shiver of Food Fear run down my back. No tongue sandwiches will be touching my tongue – and this is not said tongue-in-cheek (excuse the pun). From the first moment I saw tongue, complete with taste-buds, I knew I could never go there.

However, the Jewish Princess's calendar is filled with many other wonderful foods, and, just like the Jewish Princess's larder, it is always full to the brim, what with all the holidays, celebrations and the odd dinner-party feast thrown in. Hardly a month goes by without an excuse to make a special dish, whisk up a favourite dessert or smell the *yom tov* (holiday) cake baking in the oven. At certain times of the year I have a calling – and this isn't just when my fancy-dress outfit has arrived for Purim! This yearning makes me rekindle my love for certain dishes, and even though I could eat them all year round, I don't – a bit like wearing white jeans.

In April, I meet up and enjoy a spring fling with coconut macaroons and matzo *brie* during the eight days of Passover (see page 28). Early summer sees me marching into the supermarket to celebrate Shavuot, picking up tubs and tubs of cream cheese to whisk up my JP favourite Mars Bar Cheesecake (page 60). At the end of the summer I can't wait for my brief encounter with apples, dipping them into honey to honour a sweet Jewish New Year. After that, I keep slicing slivers of Honey Cake (page 81) until I have eaten the whole thing; even then I continue to bake more and keep slivering away until the end of Yom Kippur ten days later.

On Yom Kippur (the Day of Atonement,) I break my fast on foods that are salty but nice, such as anchovies and herrings. While they are totally unsuitable after fasting and not drinking a drop of liquid for twenty-five hours (I always go to bed with serious heartburn), as long as they're accompanied by endless, thirst-quenching cups of tea – AND MORE HONEY CAKE – I know I've made it to another year!

Just when you thought the holidays were over, like a London bus, three more turn up: Succot (page 84), Shemini Atzeret, and to finish off, Simchat Torah. This gives me just enough time to recover and then look forward to Princess Present Week, otherwise known as Chanukkah (page 102).

Of course, in between all the Jewish holidays there are so many other reasons to celebrate, from birthday parties (another JP favourite) to dinner parties and even the occasional wedding, bar mitzvah or *bris*. Before you know it, the year has come and gone in a festival of FOOD!

Yes, all the tastes of the year have a special place in my heart (please never try to feed me heart, though: I just couldn't) and being reintroduced to them again and again really does make each and every day special. So I have many treats in store for you within the following pages, and as you read, please ENJOY.

I hope that now that I have made a successful *shiddach*, you will be very happy indeed.

I
festivals

purim
the festival of lots

If ever a festival celebrated a Jewish Princess, Purim has to be it. This epic tale of blockbuster proportions really does prove that a Jewish Princess can change the course of history.

Now, you may never have thought of Queen Esther as a JP, but here is my evidence. First, although she was tragically orphaned as a child and brought up by her Uncle Mordecai, this did not stop her from getting ahead. With her Princess Positive attitude, she followed her uncle's advice, keeping *shtoom* that she was a JP (well, the king wouldn't want to know about her shopping habits) and entered the royal Persian beauty contest to replace the king's first wife, Vashti, with a younger, more beautiful model (some things never change). She took first place and the *shiddach* was made. Esther had gone from Jewish Princess to QUEEN.

I wonder if she got a bigger ring?

In her new life at court, she did not forget Mordecai – in fact, quite the opposite. When he came to her with news that Haman, the king's chief advisor, was plotting to murder the Jewish people, she knew she had to help. The lots* had literally been thrown (thus the festival of lots), and the date for the massacre set.

For three days Esther prepared at her peril to enter the king's inner court. To do this, she detoxed (fasted) and, I presume, had her hair and nails done. When the king saw her, she was welcomed (obviously she had a good hairdresser) and what did she do? She invited the king and Haman to dinner.

As any JP knows, the way to a man's heart is through his stomach.

*Lots was an actual game played by throwing stones.

Once the king and Haman had enjoyed her fabulous banquet (I bet she over-catered), Esther told the king of Haman's terrible plot and revealed that she was, in fact, a Jewish Princess. She didn't make a *megillah* (song and dance) about it, even though when we read the story of Purim, it is read from a scroll called a *megillah*. The king, like any man whose JP wife has given him a *misha bayruch* (telling off), realized he should do exactly what he was told. Therefore, justice was served: Haman was put to death and Mordecai, in true Jewish tradition, followed into the family business, becoming the king's chief advisor.

Every year this festival is celebrated in true JP style, and it is customary to get dressed up (not a Princess Problem), have parties, eat sweet triangular pastries known as *Hamantaschen* (representing the three corners of Haman's hat; see page 24), give gifts of chocolate and cake to friends and family (known as *mishloach manot*) and even to get a little *shiker*.

What better way to remember Queen Esther, an *Eshet Chayil*: a woman of worth, and a true Jewish Princess?

What did the Jewish Princess do for Purim?

She put on her new, fancy dress!

drunken fish

serves 4

400ml vegetable stock
8 lemon sole fillets, skinless, approximately 140g each
salt to taste
2 tablespoons Chinese cooking wine
1 red Thai chilli (use less if you don't like it too spicy)
a few slices of grated fresh ginger
4 spring onions, only the white part, cut horizontally
10g chopped fresh coriander

In a large pan, bring the stock to the boil, then reduce the heat so that it simmers.

Wash and season the sole with a little salt.

Add the Chinese cooking wine to the stock, along with the chilli, ginger and onions. Cook, stirring occasionally, for 1 minute.

Add the chopped coriander and the fish to the stock mixture. Continue cooking until the fish is cooked.

Why not get dressed up Chinese-style (I love Shanghai Tang) and serve with rice and chopsticks?

a shissel of shikerer chicken

serves 6

3–4 tablespoons olive oil (depending on the size of chicken)
2 onions, diced
1 large chicken, cut into 8 pieces
100g plain flour
75cl white wine
1 x 400g tin chopped tomatoes
500ml boiled water
1 tablespoon vegetable stock powder
120g jar of sliced black olives
1 teaspoon dried oregano
salt and black pepper to taste

Pour the oil in a frying pan and fry the onions until slightly brown. Transfer into a large *shissel*, or cooking pot.

Roll each piece of chicken in the plain flour, then fry in the olive oil until lightly brown and place in the *shissel*.

Pour in the wine and let it cook for approximately 1 minute, then add the tomatoes, water, stock powder, olives, oregano and salt and black pepper to taste. Bring to the boil and simmer for 1 hour.

Remove the chicken from the *shissel* and turn up the heat. Stir continuously while the sauce reduces to ensure that it doesn't burn. Cook for 10–15 minutes, or until you can see a difference in volume.

Pour the thickened sauce over the chicken. Cook, covered, in an oven preheated to 180°C/350°F/gas mark 4 for 15 minutes.

A tasty way of eating chicken, but make sure the children don't get shiker!

jerk burgers

makes approximately 16

1kg minced turkey
1½ dessertspoons jerk spice
1 large egg
2 tablespoons matzo meal
vegetable oil for frying
1 x 430g tin sliced pineapple rings in their own juice
juice of 1½ limes
iceberg lettuce
16 small burger baps (small round bridge rolls are better)

Mix the first four jerk burger ingredients together. Moisten your hands with water, take a large tablespoon of the mixture and form it into a patty. Repeat until you have 16.

Fry the patties on each side for 5–10 minutes, until golden brown.

When ready to serve, put the pineapple rings and their juice in a large saucepan. Add the lime juice and heat through.

Strain away the juice, then place one pineapple ring under each burger and serve with the iceberg lettuce on the baps.

A burger to spice up your life.

prune and chocolate hamantaschen

makes approximately 40

for the filling
200g dark chocolate
140g soft dried prunes
2 tablespoons sour cream
1 tablespoon brandy

for the pastry
250g softened unsalted butter
80g light brown sugar
2 large egg yolks
400g plain flour, sifted
1 teaspoon baking powder
3 tablespoons smooth (no pulp) orange juice

Preheat the oven to 180°C/350°F/gas mark 4.

First, make the filling. Break the chocolate into squares and place them in a double-saucepan (bain-marie) or in a small, heatproof bowl over a pan of hot water to melt.

Once melted, remove the chocolate from the heat and add the rest of the filling ingredients. Blend until very smooth.

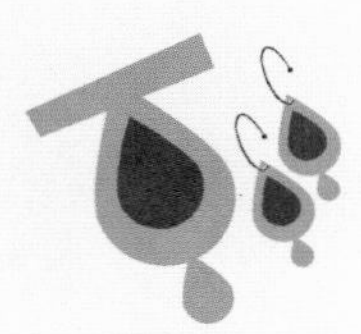

To make the pastry, beat the butter and sugar together until pale.

While still beating, slowly add the egg yolks to the mixture one at a time.

Still beating, add spoonfuls of the dry ingredients until all used up.

Continue to beat until this is all incorporated, then slowly add the orange juice.

On a very well-floured board, pat out the pastry with your hands to approximately 5mm in thickness.

With a 7cm cookie cutter, cut the pastry into circles and place them on a baking tray lined with baking parchment.

Moisten the edges of each circle (do one at a time) with water, then place a teaspoonful of the chocolate mixture in the centre of each. Fold in the edges to form a triangular shape.

Bake for approximately 15–20 minutes, or until the pastry is a pale golden brown.

Cool in the baking tray on a wire rack before serving.

A wickedly delicious treat.

fritlach

makes approximately 30

240g plain flour
1 egg
¼ teaspoon salt
1 tablespoon vegetable oil
about 4 tablespoons water
1 tablespoon runny honey
vegetable oil for frying
caster sugar

Put all the ingredients except the vegetable oil for frying and the caster sugar into a mixer or food processor. Blend until you have a soft dough.

Dust a chopping board with flour and knead the dough on it for about 1 minute.

Cover with cling film and refrigerate for 30 minutes.

Remove the dough from the fridge and roll it out on a well-floured board until it is paper-thin.

Use a biscuit cutter and cut it into rounds, or if you wish, cut it into crescents or use your artistic flair and create other shapes.

Fry the shapes in the vegetable oil until pale golden brown on each side (this takes only a few seconds).

Place on kitchen paper to absorb any excess oil, then sprinkle with the caster sugar.

A golden moment, best served hot.

posh pears

serves 6–8

8 large pears (*i.e.* Williams)
peeled, but with stalks left on
juice of half a lemon
800ml red wine
170g caster sugar
2 cinnamon sticks
1 vanilla pod, split lengthwise

Put the pears in a deep saucepan and drizzle them with the lemon juice.

Mix the red wine with the caster sugar and pour over the pears.

Place the cinnamon sticks and vanilla pod in the liquid.

Bring to the boil and simmer for approximately 40 minutes, or until the pears are soft. Keep turning the pears during this procedure to make sure they cook evenly.

When the pears are ready, remove them from the saucepan and leave them to cool in a serving dish.

Place the lid on the saucepan and boil the rest of the ingredients on a high heat until the liquid has reduced by half and looks like a thick syrup.

Strain and pour over the pears.

A dessert beyond com-pear!

the princess perfect passover

Before every Passover, a Jewish Princess always asks herself three very important questions:

> Who is going to make Seder?
> Answer: Me.
> Who is going to clean out all the cupboards?
> Answer: Me.
> Who is going to fight her way around the supermarket?
> Answer: Me.

This is quickly followed by a fourth very important question:

> Can we go away this year?

Each year, before you know it, Passover descends upon us. You can feel it in the air: a change of mood, worry and anxiety. Questions are asked – and these are not the ones in the *Hagaddah*, the book that tells the story of Passover. Who is going to make the Seder? This is a two-day annual event: a feast where we sit around the table, which is dressed in a white table cloth and holding the Seder plate*, and drink cups of kiddush wine and continue the tradition of retelling the story of the exodus from Egypt.

Yes, we were slaves unto Egypt and we had had enough of bondage (I won't make a joke here). We escaped from persecution with the help of Moses and the Main Man, together with many miracles. Because of this, our JP ancestors made a speedy exit, leaving Egypt behind, to

*The plate of symbolic foods used at Passover.

wander in the desert for forty years. It was so speedy, in fact, that they had no time to let their bread rise (they didn't have electric bread-makers in those days); they simply carried the dough on their backs and it baked in the sun. So during Passover we eat unleavened bread, called matzo: a large, dry, FAT-FREE cracker.

Every Jewish Princess has to decide just how Princess Passover she is prepared to be. I mean, there is so much to do, from spring cleaning (personally, I love a bit of Passover feng shui) to 'Changing Over'. Changing Over means just that: changing over all your crockery, cutlery, saucepans, utensils, etc., to a whole new set that can be used only for Passover (a good excuse to hit the homeware department). Some Princesses line every surface of their kitchens, and others even have a kitchen that they open up just to use during Passover. Cupboards are emptied, and traditionally foods that you are not able to use during the holiday (these foods are called *chametz*) are sold for a token amount and then usually passed on to charity. So all new food is bought that has been cooked under supervision. You can recognize these foods because they all have a special label (I love a label) which shows they are *Pesachdic* – designed for Passover, that is, not Prada.

I have to confess that it is not only the preparation for Passover but actually the *keeping* of it that makes me ask, should I pass over Passover? I just can't help it, even when I know I'm not afraid of a little hard work – though I know you don't believe me. I love it when the house has been spring-cleaned (OK, so I have had a little *help*...). And I don't mind clearing out kitchen cupboards: it can be quite therapeutic, actually, and I always find something that is out of date. If I'm really honest with myself, sitting down for Seder night is one of the most special evenings of the year, and it gives me a strong sense of who I am and where I come from.

Yes, even the food during Passover can be fantastic, but my advice? Go easy on the eggs. I mean, you haven't lived until you have tried a hard-boiled egg in salt water (I know: it sounds disgusting), and as for coconut macaroons and cinnamon balls, these delicious sweetmeats should be eaten all year round.

But of course they're not.

I mean, it would be like eating Christmas pudding in August.

So now I have one more question to ask. Why do I panic at Passover? I suppose it's the *thought* of Passover that scares me (anyone else feel the same?) Yet, looking on the bright side, it's only eight days – not forty years! Your house is immaculate. Your Seder night will provide you and your children with wonderful memories, and with the help of my wonderful recipes for breakfast, savoury dishes and of course, some Princess Passover sweet treats, just think of this festival as getting in touch with all those wonderful traditions that have been passed down from generation to generation.

This year I am going to make it a Princess Positive Passover, and you never know: maybe next year we'll be in Jerusalem.

Personally, though, I would like to be at the Royal Beach – in Eilat!

princess passover pointers

1. Princess Prepare. Making lists is invaluable. Mine are always very long!

2. When spring arrives, start using up everything in your larder, your second larder and ALL your freezers.

3. Need to use up alcohol? Have a pre-Passover party, or donate booze to your local university or even your gardener (once he has finished).

4. Received any dodgy wedding presents or gifts that aren't quite Princess Perfect? Keep them for Passover. When it comes to style, just think 'eclectic'.

5. Glass bowls, etc., can be used for cold milk or meat meals, so if buying new, GO FOR GLASS.

6. To line your kitchen cupboards, buy laminated material. Use tracing paper to make templates of your shelves, then use those to cut out the material.

7. Join a cash-and-carry. Disposable plates, etc., make life a lot easier, especially if you're greeted with one, two or ten extra guests (like when the kids invite 'just a few' of their friends over). It may not be environmentally friendly, but it will make *you* friendlier – and you can always recycle.

8. Try to Princess Plan your meals for all eight days of Passover so that you'll order all the correct ingredients.

9. If you are invited to a Princess Pal's for dinner, take a lovely present and GO!

10. Even though the story of Passover is all about slavery, use the above Princess Pointers and make sure you are *not* a slave to your kitchen.

bobbie bagels

makes approximately 24

180g non-dairy margarine
500ml water
½ teaspoon salt
200g fine matzo meal
4 eggs
1 dessertspoon sugar.

Preheat the oven to 200°C/400°F/gas mark 6.

Melt the margarine in a saucepan over a low heat. Stir in all the other ingredients until the mixture resembles a choux-like dough.

Moisten your hands with water. Take a heaped dessertspoon of the dough at a time and form it into a ball.

Place the bagels on a baking tray lined with parchment paper.

Make a hole in the centre of each.

Bake for approximately 30–35 minutes, or until lightly browned on top.

Perfect for lunch-boxes.

bubbelehs (passover pancakes)

makes approximately 15

4 eggs
1 tablespoon milk
4 tablespoons fine matzo meal
vegetable oil for frying
4 tablespoons caster sugar
1 teaspoon cinnamon

In a medium bowl, mix the eggs, milk and matzo meal together until the mixture is smooth.

Heat the oil in a large frying pan.

Drop a tablespoon of the mixture at a time into the hot oil. Repeat until the pan is full.

Fry the pancakes until golden brown – this should take only a couple of minutes – turning them over halfway through the cooking time to make sure the colour is even.

When golden brown all over, turn out onto kitchen roll to remove any excess oil.

In a separate bowl, mix together the sugar and cinnamon.

When the *bubbelehs* are ready to eat, serve with the cinnamon sugar on the side, ready for dipping.

For a more sophisticated alternative, use a tablespoon of sweet red wine instead of milk.

matzo brie

serves 2

4 large matzos
3 large eggs
100ml full-fat milk
unsalted butter
2 tablespoons caster sugar

Break up the matzos into small pieces and place them in a large bowl.

Beat the eggs and add the milk. Stir the mixture and pour it over the broken matzos. Leave to soak for 5 minutes.

Coat a large frying pan with melted butter and pour in the saturated matzo mixture.

Cook over a low heat for a few minutes and turn over halfway through cooking. It will look similar to an omelette.

Divide the mixture in two and place each half on a plate.

Sprinkle each matzo *brie* with caster sugar to serve.

JP Junior's grandpa prefers it with salt, and JP Junior's brother prefers it with ketchup. You choose!

princess passover granola

makes approximately 8 large portions

150g matzo
6 tablespoons runny honey
100g hazelnuts
100g chopped walnuts
100g prunes
150g raisins
150g dried chopped apricots
100g dried chopped dates

Bash the matzo into very, very small pieces.

In a frying pan, mix together the matzo crumbs and honey. Cook over a low heat until the matzo is thoroughly coated with the honey.

Mix the honeyed matzo with the hazelnuts and chopped walnuts and place under a hot grill. Toast for 2 minutes, stirring occasionally so that the mixture doesn't burn.

Cool, then add the dried fruit and stir well. Store in an airtight container until ready to serve.

I have never been able to find a delicious cereal to eat during Passover, so I devised this wonderful granola, guaranteed to make a Princess Perfect Passover. Cover with milk or add to yoghurt and fruit. This cereal is so good that you might consider crunching on it all year round.

A word about gefilte fish

If gefilte fish were a football team, it would be playing in division four. However, it would definitely have a very loyal fan base, which would either have loved it since childhood or developed a taste for it somewhere along the way.

Admittedly, this very unusual boiled or fried minced fish is not to everyone's taste. Even the orange and grey-white outfit (a bit like my washing) with a splash of deep purple that gefilte fish would play in would not be to everyone's taste. But like all underdogfish, gefilte fish can sometimes be a true winner. I can hear its fans shouting from the sidelines: 'Go, 'Filte Fish, Go!'

Whether traditionally made from minced white fish and matzo meal, boiled and served with a fish liqueur and a topping of sliced boiled carrot, or fried golden brown and served with a side of *chrayn* (a hot, purple-coloured horseradish sauce), gefilte fish is a true delicacy.

I have developed a taste for gefilte fish and I am an ardent supporter of this strange, badly dressed fishy dish. However, it *has* to be fresh. I am afraid that buying boiled fish in a jar, as you often find it, is simply fake fish. I really think that, if handled in the right way, gefilte fish can take on the big boys and be a real winner.

If I were the manager of this football team, my one piece of advice, when dealing with gefilte fish, would be 'Handle with care'. If not treated with kid gloves – or, in gefilte fish's case, rubber – you could be left with a stink on your hands that simply will *not* go away.

gefilte fish

makes approximately 85 mini gefilte fish balls

2 litres vegetable stock (made with 2 tablespoons stock powder)
4 carrots, peeled
2 onions, peeled and left whole
1 tablespoon caster sugar
900g minced fish (equal amounts of whiting, haddock and bream)
2 tablespoons sugar
1 teaspoon salt
1 onion, finely grated
2 eggs
80g fine matzo meal
a sprinkle of white pepper

Combine the stock, carrots, onions and sugar in a large saucepan. Bring to the boil and simmer for approximately 15 minutes, or until the carrots begin to soften.

While this is cooking, put the rest of the gefilte fish ingredients in a food processor and mix well.

With damp hands (use a bowl of water for dipping), take a teaspoon of mixture and roll it into small balls, then place these in the simmering stock. Cover and cook for approximately 10 minutes, or until the gefilte fish balls are cooked through.

Remove the balls with a slotted spoon and leave to cool in a colander.

Keep the stock simmering for a further 20 minutes to reduce.

Remove the carrots and slice them into thin discs.

Pour the remaining stock through a sieve and leave to cool.

Place the gefilte fish balls into a serving dish, pour the liquor over them and place a piece of carrot on top of each fish ball.

Serve warm or cold with *chrayn*.

If you wish to fry the fish balls, place into hot vegetable oil and fry until golden brown. Don't forget to put on your extractor fan!

This dish works equally well as an appetizer. Just remember not to confuse them with your matzo balls and put them in the chicken soup…

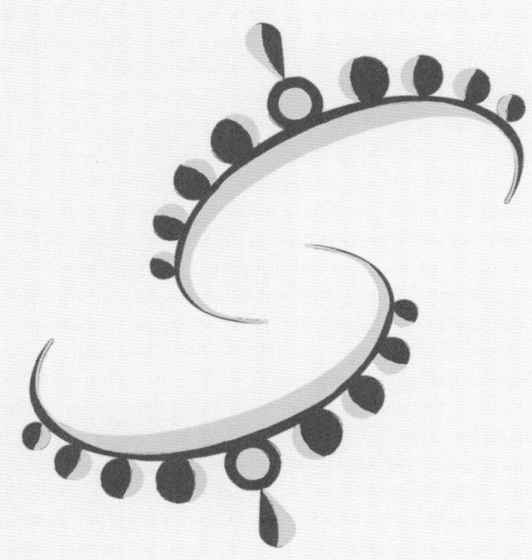

matzo meat parcels

serves 6

for the parcel
10 matzos
water
110ml olive oil

for the filling
2 onions
2 garlic cloves, peeled and chopped
3 tablespoons olive oil
400g (about 2) potatoes, sliced very thin
1kg minced beef
1 aubergine, diced
salt and black pepper, to taste
80g sultanas
300ml beef stock (reserve 100ml for the top of the pie), made with one beef stock cube
10g chopped flat-leaf parsley
1 teaspoon cinnamon
2 large eggs
2 tablespoons fine matzo meal

Preheat the oven to 180°C/350°F/gas mark 4.

First, make the parcel. Take the matzos and dip each one for a few seconds in cold water to soften them, then wrap them in a tea towel for approximately 15 minutes.

Meanwhile, make the filling. Fry the onions and garlic in the olive oil until soft and translucent.

Add the potatoes and continue frying. When they are slightly brown, add the meat and the aubergine.

Season to taste with salt and black pepper.

After approximately 10 minutes, add the sultanas and 200ml of the beef stock, the cinnamon and parsley.

Stir and continue cooking until the meat is done – approximately 20 minutes.

Remove from the heat and stir in the eggs and matzo meal. Check the seasoning and adjust it if necessary.

Grease a 20cm loose-bottomed tin. Brush each matzo with a thin coating of olive oil on each side, then use them to line the bottom and sides of tin. Don't worry if the matzos stick out the top; this will be used for the top of the parcel. Save two matzos for the middle of the top.

Pour the filling into the parcel, and then close the parcel with the two reserved matzos and any matzo sticking out of the top.

Bake in the preheated oven for approximately 25 minutes, then remove and pour in the 100ml of reserved stock to moisten the top of the parcel. Return to the oven for a further 5 minutes.

Remove and cut around the sides. Then – and this is the best part – release your parcel from its tin and serve.

A gift of a dish for a Passover Princess.

rosemary and lemon chicken

serves 4–6

1 chicken, cut into pieces
1 bunch of spring onions, roughly chopped
1 large sprig of rosemary
1 small bunch of thyme
1 small bunch of basil
juice and grated rind of 1 lemon
salt and black pepper
a little water for basting

Preheat the oven to 180°C/350°F/gas mark 4.

Place the chicken in a roasting dish.

Add the rest of the ingredients, seasoning to taste with the salt and pepper.

Cook for approximately 1 hour, turning the chicken halfway through and basting from time to time.

A summery chicken dish that has a Mediterranean feel. Personally, I always like to feel that I am in the Mediterranean!

cinnamon baubles

makes approximately 45

2 egg whites
200g ground almonds
180g caster sugar
1 dessertspoon cinnamon
1 dessertspoon *kiddush* wine
100g icing sugar

Preheat the oven to 170°C/325°F/gas mark 3.

Whisk the egg whites until stiff.

Add all the other ingredients except the icing sugar, and whisk until the mixture resembles a paste.

Moisten your hands with water and roll the mixture into small balls – roughly the size of a very, very large diamond or a walnut.

Place the baubles on a baking tray lined with parchment paper and bake for approximately 12 minutes, or until a light golden-brown.

Remove from the oven and leave to cool, but not completely.

While still slightly warm, place the baubles in a plastic bag, add the icing sugar and shake – the cinnamon baubles will turn diamond white!

When completely cold, store in an airtight container.

I have to say I haven't tasted better than these, but see what you think. A gem of a cinnamon bauble!

coconutties

makes approximately 12

5 egg yolks
150g caster sugar
150g desiccated coconut
150g mixed dried fruit with chocolate drops
100g plain dark chocolate

Preheat the oven to 180°C/350°F/gas mark 4.

Beat the egg yolks with the sugar until pale.

Add the rest of the ingredients except the plain chocolate.

Moisten your hands with water. Take a dessertspoon of the mixture and mould it into a pyramid shape with a flat bottom.

Place the pyramids on a baking sheet and bake in the preheated oven for 10–15 minutes. Leave to cool on a wire rack.

When the coconutties are cold, melt the plain chocolate in a double saucepan (bain-marie), or use a heatproof bowl over a saucepan filled with simmering water.

Dip the bottom of the biscuits in the chocolate and place on a wire rack to set. Drizzle any leftover chocolate over the coconutties.

When baking the biscuits, put them on a low rack in the oven to prevent the tops from going brown. Store (if there are any left) in an airtight container.

grandma's matzo pudding

serves 10

7 large matzos
200g caster sugar
4 eggs
120g non-dairy margarine, melted
60g ground almonds
150ml *kiddush* wine
1 cooking apple, peeled and grated
140g sultanas
100g chopped walnuts
2 tablespoon chocolate powder
1 tablespoon cinnamon

for the topping
2 tablespoons caster sugar
1 handful walnut pieces

Preheat the oven to 150°C/300°F/gas mark 2.

Break the matzos into bite-sized pieces and wet them in a colander. When soggy, squeeze out any excess water.

Mix the matzo pieces together with all other ingredients.

Grease an ovenproof dish, approximately 22cm square by 5cm deep, pour in the matzo mixture.

Mix the topping ingredients together and sprinkle over the pudding.

Bake for approximately 45 minutes.

I was so excited when I discovered my grandma's recipe. It is absolutely delicious: a JP Passover version of bread pudding. You could fuel marathon runners on this wonderful dessert – or become a marathon runner yourself if you eat too much…

'must-have' macaroons

makes approximately 35

3 egg whites
250g ground almonds
250g caster sugar
1 teaspoon almond essence
150g bashed flaked almonds (I advise using a rolling pin to bash flaked almonds)

Preheat the oven to 180°C/350°F/gas mark 4.

Whisk the egg whites until stiff.

Fold in the ground almonds and caster sugar. Add the almond essence. At this stage the mixture will form a paste.

Spread the bashed almonds on a flat surface. Moisten your hands in some water, take a teaspoon of the mixture and roll it into a ball.

Roll the marzipan ball in the almonds and place it on a baking tray covered in parchment paper. Leave space between the macaroons as they spread when cooking.

Bake in the preheated oven for 10 minutes.

Remove from the oven, leave to cool and harden. As the week progresses, the macaroons will harden, so my advice is eat ASAP!

These upmarket trendy bites are delicious all year round – not just Passover – and can even be served as a petit four.

princess plava

serves 8

5 large eggs, separated
275g caster sugar
(divided roughly in half)
finely grated rind of 1 lemon
and 1 tablespoon of its juice
75g cake matzo meal
75g fine matzo meal

Preheat the oven to 180°C/350°F/gas mark 4.

Whisk the egg whites until stiff, then slowly add half the sugar (approximately 140g).

In a separate bowl, beat the egg yolks and add the other half of the sugar (135g). Mix until the mixture turns pale, then add the lemon juice.

Very slowly add the egg-white mixture to the egg-yolk mixture.

Add both matzo meals, tablespoon by tablespoon, to the cake mixture.

Fold in the finely grated lemon rind.

Place in a lined 23cm loose-bottomed cake tin and bake for approximately 1 hour. Cool before serving.

A light and fluffy cake. Princess Plava Perfect, of course!

shavuot

festival of weeks/pentecost

Shavuot commemorates the giving of the Torah to Moses on Mount Sinai. This was the first time the rules of *kashrus* were written, so you could say that when the Ten Commandments were given and the rules of *kashrus* received, the first Diet Bible was published, quite literally, in stone. It's amazing how many JPs have stuck to the rules ever since. Who says we have no willpower?

Our Princess ancestors must have been incredibly resourceful; after all, travelling through the desert is hard enough, never mind then being handed a whole new set of rules to govern your life. I can't imagine being stuck in the desert without a five-star hotel and a credit card (mind you, I can't imagine being *anywhere* without a credit card). While busy organizing their new kosher kitchens, separating milk and meat with different crockery, cutlery and cooking utensils, those early Jewish Princesses avoided any culinary confusion by eating only milk meals – which is why, during the festival of Shavuot, it is customary to eat dairy foods.

When the Torah was given by G-d* (like a bridegroom) to the bride (the Jewish people), it is said that Mount Sinai resembled the *chuppah* (the marriage canopy) and miraculously blossomed with flowers and foliage. So to make yourself feel like a true Dairy Queen, it is customary to fill your home with flowers and plants. You could even use this tradition as a good excuse to put in your order with your favourite florist.

I simply adore dairy dishes, and when it comes to Shavuot, it is my commandment to forget the calories, raid the cheese counter and bring out the blintzes (see page 56). Of course, the Princess *pièce de resistance* is to cut a large slice or two of cheesecake. So in this chapter, follow my culinary rules and enjoy my top-ten dairy dishes. If you fancy adding your own Princess touch, go ahead. After all, *my* recipes are *not* set in stone!

*A JP writes G-d like this because she was taught never to take G-d's name in vain, even in writing.

potatoes lyonnaise

serves 8

450ml double cream
1 large pinch ground nutmeg
2 teaspoons garlic purée
salt and black pepper to taste
butter for greasing
850g potatoes, peeled and thinly sliced
3 onions, peeled and thinly sliced

Preheat the oven to 180°C/350°F/gas mark 4.

In a large bowl, mix together the cream, nutmeg, garlic purée and salt and pepper.

Grease an ovenproof dish. I use a glass one (19cm x 8cm) so you can see the layered potato.

Put in a layer of potato slices, then a layer of onions, then cover with some of the cream mixture. Repeat this until you have used up all the ingredients; I make three layers, finishing with the cream mixture.

Cover and bake in the preheated oven for approximately 1–1½ hours.

A little bit of French decadence. That's why I love French designer dishes!

princess spinach

serves 6

3 finely chopped shallots
2 tablespoons olive oil
500g fresh spinach leaves, well-washed
30g butter
60g pine nuts, lightly toasted in a dry frying pan
salt and black pepper
30g chopped Parmesan

In a large frying pan, fry the shallots in the olive oil until soft.

Add the spinach leaves and butter. Cook until the leaves wilt (this takes very little time).

Add the pine nuts and seasoning to taste.

Finally, add the Parmesan, stir, and serve.

Perfect as a 'post-pump-class' treat.

spinach and ricotta flan

serves 10

375g short-crust pastry (ready-rolled)
baking beans
1 teaspoon olive oil
1 small red onion, diced
500g fresh spinach, well-washed
500g ricotta cheese
salt and pepper to taste
1 teaspoon nutmeg
a handful of pine nuts

Preheat the oven to 190°C/375°F/gas mark 5.

Roll out the pastry to 5mm and place it in a flan dish approximately 30cm in diameter. Prick the pastry all over with a fork. Line it with greaseproof paper and fill it with baking beans. Bake the pastry for 10 minutes. Leave to cool, then remove the baking beans.

Heat the oil in a frying pan and fry the onions until soft. Transfer them to a mixing bowl.

Put the spinach in the frying pan and cook until wilted. Transfer to a colander and let all the water drain away.

Put the spinach in the mixing bowl with the onions, then add the ricotta, salt and pepper, and nutmeg. Mix well.

Pour the mixture into the pastry case. Sprinkle with the pine nuts and bake in the preheated oven for approximately 25–30 minutes. Serve hot or cold.

Flan-tastic!

strawberry, feta and toasted pecan salad

serves 8

for the salad
60g pecans
1 tablespoon light brown sugar
8 strawberries, sliced
100g feta cheese, crumbled
1 iceberg or romaine lettuce, shredded

for the dressing
2 tablespoons olive oil
1 tablespoon white-wine vinegar
2 tablespoons low-fat yoghurt
1 teaspoon caster sugar
½ teaspoon Dijon mustard
salt and black pepper

In a dry frying pan, stir the pecans in the sugar over a medium heat until the nuts are well-coated.

Toss all the salad ingredients in a bowl.

Mix together all the dressing ingredients.

Dress the salad just before serving.

A super summer salad full of goodies.

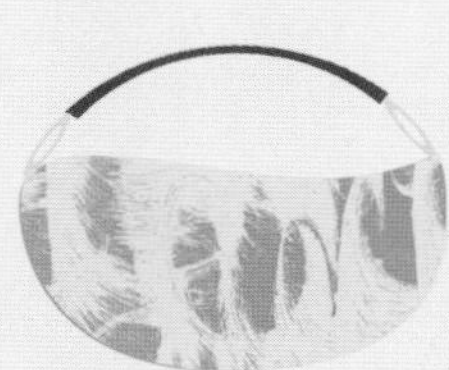

vegetable risotto

serves 2 as a main dish, 4 as a side dish

1 tablespoon olive oil
2 shallots, finely chopped
2 garlic cloves, finely chopped
225g arborio risotto rice
1 litre vegetable stock
1 red pepper, finely chopped
6 chestnut mushrooms, sliced
20g unsalted butter
salt and black pepper to taste

In a large saucepan, slowly heat the vegetable stock over a low heat and keep it simmering. In another saucepan, heat the olive oil and fry the shallots and garlic until soft.

Add the rice to the shallots and garlic and cook, stirring, for approximately 2 minutes. Add a ladle of stock and keep stirring until the rice has absorbed the stock. Keep doing this until you have used half the stock.

Add the red pepper, mushrooms, salt and pepper. Continue adding the stock, one ladle-ful at a time. Once the stock has all been used up, the risotto should be ready. It should look creamy, and the rice will be cooked but still retain a slight bite.

Check and adjust the seasoning, if necessary. Add the butter and serve.

I've always been fascinated by risotto: it is so creamy and delicious. By using the two saucepans you will get a Princess Perfect risotto – and it is so easy!

coconut rice pudding

serves 8

140g short-grained pudding rice
55g light brown sugar
750ml milk
300ml coconut milk
(I use reduced-fat)

Preheat the oven to 150°C/300°F/gas mark 2.

Grease an ovenproof dish that will hold 1.3 litres.

Place all ingredients in the dish and bake for 1 hour and 20 minutes.

I love this dessert. However, for some pupils – I mean, people – seeing this pudding brought to the table transports them back to their school dining hall. I cannot guarantee that their first experience of rice pudding was a good one, however, so better make two desserts – just in case.

cherry cheese blintzes

makes approximately 24

for the blintzes
500g plain flour
4 large eggs
1.2 litres full-fat milk
olive oil for frying

for the cherry syrup
400ml syrup (reserved from jar)
6 tablespoons caster sugar

for the filling
300g mascarpone cheese
200g cream cheese
2 tablespoons caster sugar
1 egg yolk
1 pinch salt
1 x 680g jar morello cherries in syrup, drained (reserve 400ml syrup)

First make the blintzes (pancakes) by mixing together all the blintz ingredients, except the oil, in a blender. Leave it in the fridge for at least half an hour or, even better, overnight.

When the mixture is ready, make the filling by mixing together all the filling ingredients, leaving the cherries until last and carefully folding them in.

Whisk the batter before using to ensure a good consistency. Coat a 20cm round, thin frying pan by pouring the oil into it and swirling it around the pan, then pouring out any excess and wiping around the pan with kitchen paper.

Heat the coated frying pan and pour in a thin layer of batter. The pancake is ready when the mixture starts to bubble or come away from the side. When that happens, just flip it over to brown it lightly. The first pancake is normally a disaster, so don't worry – just eat it!

Turn the pancakes out onto a baking sheet and leave to cool. Continue this method, but keep oiling the pan after every two pancakes.

the blintz

Preheat the oven to 190°C/375°F/gas mark 5.

Take one blintz and fill it with approximately 1 tablespoon of the filling mixture. Roll up the blintz and fold both sides underneath to create a parcel. Place in an ovenproof dish. Continue this process until the dish is filled.

Bake the blintzes in the preheated oven for approximately 15 minutes, or until lightly browned.

While the blintzes are baking, put the cherry syrup and sugar in a small saucepan. Bring to the boil and let bubble for approximately 15 minutes, or until the syrup has reduced and thickened.

Serve your blintzes with the cherry sauce drizzled over the top.

For extra calories, a lovely dollop of sour cream on the side makes this cherry-cheese blintz THE BUSINESS!

chocolate duo-oh-oh-oh!

serves 8

for the coffee-chocolate mousse
100g coffee chocolate
2 eggs, separated
100ml double cream

for the milk-chocolate mousse
200g good milk chocolate
3 eggs, separated
150ml double cream

for the decoration
Grated chocolate of choice (mine is white)

Note: You'll need 8 individual coffee cups (bone china, of course!) This is best made the day before.

Slowly melt the dark-coffee chocolate in a double saucepan (bain-marie), or use a small heatproof bowl placed over a saucepan of simmering water. When the chocolate has melted, remove it from the heat. Stir in the egg yolks, followed by the cream.

Whisk the egg whites until stiff, then fold into the mixture. Put into a jug and then pour into coffee cups, filling each ¼ of the way up. Refrigerate.

Repeat the whole process with the milk-chocolate mousse ingredients and pour this on top of the dark coffee-chocolate mousse up to the top of each coffee cup.

Grate on your chocolate of choice. Refrigerate until set.

Perfect for dinner parties. Junior JPs love it made with milk chocolate.

chocolate sour cream cake

serves 8

180g plain chocolate digestive biscuits
60g butter, melted
100g dark chocolate
2 eggs
100g caster sugar
10fl oz sour cream
100g white chocolate chips

Preheat the oven to 170°C/325°F/gas mark 3.

Put the digestive biscuits in a plastic bag, then bash them with a rolling pin. Put them in a mixer and beat together with the melted butter until the mixture looks like a paste.

Put the biscuit mixture in a greased 21cm springform cake tin and push it down with a fork to form a base. Refrigerate.

Melt the chocolate in a double saucepan (bain-marie) or use a small heatproof bowl over a saucepan full of hot water. When the chocolate has melted, remove it from the heat.

Beat the eggs and sugar together until light and fluffy. This takes a few minutes; start the mixer on slow, then speed up and don't Princess Panic. Add the sour cream and melted chocolate. Stir in the chocolate chips.

Take the cake tin out of the fridge and pour in the cake mixture. Bake for approximately 40 minutes, until the cake is set. Remove from the oven and once cool, refrigerate.

When you eat this, you will smile like the cat that got the (sour) cream.

mars bar cheesecake

serves 8

for the base
240g digestive biscuits
100g melted butter

for the topping
100g milk chocolate
150g mascarpone cheese
1 Mars bar

for the cake
300g cream cheese
100g mascarpone cheese
4 egg yolks
80g caster sugar
180ml ready-made toffee sauce

Preheat the oven to 180°C/350°F/gas mark 4.

To make the base, crush the biscuits by putting them into a bag and bashing them with a rolling pin (I recommend this after a stressful day).

Put the biscuit crumbs in a bowl and mix in the melted butter.

Grease a 20cm cake tin, then press the biscuit mixture down to form a base. Refrigerate.

Meanwhile, make the cake by whisking together all the cake ingredients except for the toffee sauce.

Pour the toffee sauce over the base of the cake and spread evenly.

Whisk the cake mixture well again, then pour it on top of the base and bake for approximately 35 minutes.

When the cake is nearly cooked, start making the topping.

Melt the milk chocolate in a double saucepan (bain-marie). If you haven't got a double saucepan, then just use a heatproof bowl over a saucepan of simmering water.

Once the chocolate has melted, add the mascarpone cheese and stir until the mixture is smooth. Remove the pan from the heat.

Remove the cake from the oven and leave to cool for approximately 10 minutes.

Spread the topping on the cake and place pieces of broken Mars bar on the top.

Leave to cool completely, then refrigerate.

A cheesecake that is out of this world! A real favourite with teenagers, so when you ask them to tidy their bedrooms, make this cake and they won't look at you as if you have arrived from Mars!

rosh hashanah & yom kippur

from feast to fast, with fast feasts

In the Jewish Princess's calendar, Rosh Hashanah, translated as 'The Head of the Year', is closely followed by Yom Kippur: The Day of Atonement. This is otherwise known as the beginning of 'honey cake season', or The High Holidays. What many people may not realize is just how 'high' these holidays really are: every Jewish Princess has the delight of enjoying not one, but two new years, because Rosh Hashanah lasts for two days!

Now, I'm all for enjoyment, but this quirk of the JP calendar also brings with it a seasonal disorder that gets into the head of every JP on the planet. Up to this point, it has slipped under the scientific radar, but once you're aware of its existence, it's really quite easy to identify by its unmistakable signs.

I only have to look in my local supermarket and see food shortages: a run on golden syrup and the disappearance of mixed spice and cinnamon from the shelves. When chatting with my Princess Pals, the topic of conversation starts to revolve around the moral conundrum of which family members to invite for lunch, dinner or tea. I also notice Princesses who no longer walk with a spring in their high heels, but rather scurry around with a look of angst on their otherwise unlined faces, clutching lists and shouting down their mobile phones while shlepping huge amounts of shopping bags (even more than a JP normally has). Yes, from the beginning of 'honey cake season' until the very end of Yom Kippur, CCD can affect even the calmest and most organized Jewish Princess.

'So what *is* CCD?' I hear you ask. 'And is there A Specialist for it?'

Here are the answers. CCD is uncommonly known as Compulsive Catering Disorder. I am sorry to inform you there is no consultant this side of Harley Street who has even heard of CCD, let alone can diagnose or cure it. But I have identified this Princess Problem and am here to put your mind at ease. In my Princess Professional opinion, you will make a full recovery, right up until Passover (see page 28), when I am afraid the symptoms will return and you will once again find yourself standing outside supermarkets half an hour before they open.

To recognize the symptoms and deal with CCD, one must only look at 'learned behaviour' (inherited from our Queen Mums) to know that it is perfectly normal to panic when your fridge isn't full and your cupboards aren't brimming over, just in case one or ten people turn up for tea. So when it comes to the high holy days, isn't it reasonable to expect this genetic behaviour to reach new heights? Therefore, don't be surprised when you have invited twenty over for lunch, thirty for tea and ten for dinner, and then you go and repeat the whole pattern by doing it again the very next day!

There is a certain amount of Princess Perverse Pleasure in inviting so many guests to one's table – or should I say tables (make sure you ring the hire company early)? I have listened to many conversations like the one below, over fruit and veg mountains as JPs unload their trolleys:

'How many have you got?'

'Sixteen.'

'Lucky you. I've got twenty.'

Then they roll their eyes and start unpacking their extortionately expensive cherries.

Well. It is a *yom tov*, after all.

spanish chicken

serves 6–8

1 chicken, cut into 8 pieces
4 medium tomatoes, cut into quarters
5 bay leaves
100g kosher turkey kabano sausages, cut into approximately 5cm pieces
1 teaspoon turmeric
½ teaspoon ginger
3 small onions, chopped
250ml chicken stock

Preheat the oven to 180°C/350°F/gas mark 4.

Put the chicken, tomatoes, bay leaves and kabanos in a roasting dish.

Mix the other ingredients into the stock and pour over the chicken.

Roast in the preheated oven for approximately 1 hour and 30 minutes.

Have a fiesta and then finish with a shluff (a Yiddish siesta).

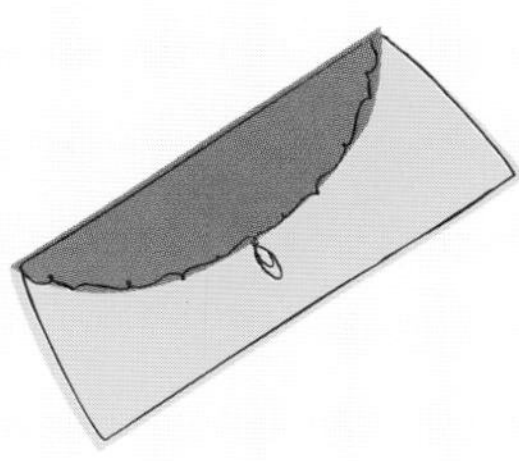

good old english roast beef with yorkshire pudding

serves 10–12

3kg ball of the (beef) rib
1 teaspoon English mustard
1 tablespoon garlic purée
4 shallots, chopped
black pepper to taste
300ml ready-made gravy
gravy granules

Preheat the oven to 180°C/350°F/gas mark 4.

Place the beef in a large roasting dish. Spread the mustard and garlic all over the meat. Arrange the shallots around the bottom of the dish. Season the meat with black pepper and pour the ready-made gravy over the meat.

Cover with foil and cook in the preheated oven for 1 hour. Remove from the oven, remove the silver foil, spoon over the juices and turn the meat over. Replace the foil and put it back in the oven to cook for another hour. If you prefer your meat well-done, I would suggest adding another half-hour to the cooking time.

When the meat has cooked, remove it from the oven and leave it to relax for 20 minutes (a bit like me), and then carve. Sieve the remaining juices into a jug and add some gravy granules (according to the instructions on the jar). Pour over the sliced meat and serve with the Yorkshire puddings on the next page.

Delicious served the next day in sandwiches with mmmmmustard.

yorkshire puddings

makes 24

olive oil for greasing
225g plain flour
2 large eggs
500ml soya milk

Preheat the oven to 200°C/400°F/gas mark 6.

Grease two muffin tins heavily with the olive oil and place them in the oven for 10 minutes while you prepare the batter.

Put the flour into a mixing bowl. Make a well in the flour, crack the eggs into the centre, then add the soya milk.

Slowly whisk the ingredients together until a batter is formed.

Remove the tins from the oven and fill each muffin tin mould up to three-quarters full.

Turn the oven down to 180°C/350°F/gas mark 4 and place the filled tins back in the oven for 15 minutes.

Carefully remove the puddings from the tins (they will be hot!) and serve with the roast beef as soon as possible.

The batter can be made the day before and stored in the fridge. Try not to eat the puddings before they go on the table!

champagne salmon

serves 4

for the fish
fresh salmon: allow 1kg for four people – this gives a generous slice for each
2 pinches of fresh dill
2 onions, peeled and sliced
400ml cava (or sparkling wine of your choice)
salt and black pepper to taste

for the crème fraîche sauce
2 teaspoon plain flour
4 tablespoons water
8 tablespoons crème fraîche
4 tablespoons sieved fish stock
2 squeezes fresh lemon juice
4 pinches dried dill
salt and black pepper to taste

Preheat the oven to 180°C/350°F/gas mark 4.

Wash the salmon well and place on a sheet of foil on a baking tray.

Add the rest of the fish ingredients, then make a loose parcel of the foil to seal in the fish. (Mine resembles a clutch bag, of course!)

Bake for approximately 10–15 minutes.

Unwrap your parcel and remove the fish with a slotted spoon, reserving the stock.

To make the sauce, mix the flour and water together in a bowl until smooth. Reserve.

In a saucepan over a low-medium heat, slowly heat the crème fraîche. Add the stock, lemon juice, dill and seasoning.

As the sauce begins to simmer, add the flour paste, turn down the heat and continue to stir for at least 1 minute.

Remove from heat, and serve the sauce with the fish.

This dish can be served hot or cold.

Fresh and fancy fish. Don't forget to serve with a glass of Princess Pink Champagne. Lechayim!

chicken marmalade

serves 6

1 chicken, cut into 8 pieces
1 onion, peeled and chopped

for the marinade
2 tablespoons thick-cut marmalade
2 teaspoons soy sauce
2 teaspoons white-wine vinegar
1 teaspoon chicken stock powder
1 sprinkle dried parsley
400ml water
salt and black pepper to taste

Preheat the oven to 180°C/350°F/gas mark 4.

Wash the chicken thoroughly and place it in an ovenproof dish, along with the chopped onion.

Mix together all marinade ingredients and pour over the chicken.

Roast in the preheated oven for approximately 45 minutes to 1 hour, basting occasionally with the marinade. The chicken is done when the juices run clear.

The chicken turns a gorgeous golden colour – rather like me after a spray tan!

celeriac and apple mash

serves 8–10

2 peeled celeriac (roughly 1kg), cut into chunks
3 eating apples (roughly 240g; I use Pink Lady), peeled and cut into chunks
150g dairy-free margarine
salt and black pepper to taste

Place the celeriac in a saucepan, cover with water and bring to the boil. Simmer until the celeriac is soft.

In a microwave, cook the apple chunks on high for approximately 5 minutes.

When the celeriac is cooked, remove it from the heat and drain, then add the apple and any apple juice that may be in the microwave cooking bowl.

Add the dairy-free margarine and season to taste with the salt and pepper.

Using a hand blender, blend all the ingredients together until the mixture is smooth.

Check and adjust the seasoning, if necessary, and serve.

Designer mash.

green beans and mushrooms

serves 8

olive oil for frying
1 large onion, diced
800g green beans, topped and tailed
400g white cup mushrooms, quartered
800g tinned chopped tomatoes
250ml extra-light olive oil
4 tablespoons tomato ketchup
1 teaspoon garlic purée
salt and black pepper to taste

In a frying pan, heat some olive oil and fry the chopped onion until it is slightly brown.

In a large saucepan, place the cooked onion, green beans, mushrooms, chopped tomatoes, oil, ketchup and garlic. Bring to the boil and simmer for approximately 1 hour.

Season to taste and serve.

A mean bean dish.

israeli salad

serves 6

4 spring onions
1½ cucumbers
2 beef tomatoes
seeds of 1 pomegranate (or, better still, get ready-prepared seeds)
1 handful of finely chopped flat-leaf parsley
grated rind and juice of 1 lemon
1 teaspoon table salt
1 tablespoon virgin olive oil

Chop all the vegetables into tiny pieces and place in a serving bowl.

Add the pomegranate, parsley, and lemon rind and juice.

Mix the salt and olive oil together and pour over the salad.

Toss well before serving.

The key to this salad is chop, chop, chop!

lime and apple slaw

serves 6

1 small white cabbage, approximately 900g, shredded
150g mixed sprouts
juice of 2 limes
3 tablespoons light mayonnaise
1 tablespoon salad cream
2 red apples, sliced very thinly

Place the shredded cabbage in a bowl, together with the mixed sprouts.

Squeeze the limes into another bowl and mix with the mayonnaise and salad cream.

Add the sliced apples to the cabbage and mix in the mayonnaise dressing.

Put in the fridge until ready to serve.

Very light and refreshing: great to munch and crunch on a hot summer's day.

princess perfect potato kugel

serves 10

6 large baking potatoes, peeled and shredded
3 large sweet potatoes, peeled and shredded
1 large onion, shredded
3 large eggs, beaten
70ml olive oil
60g fine matzo meal
65g caster sugar
1 teaspoon of salt
black pepper to taste

Preheat the oven to 190°C/375°F/gas mark 5.

Place the grated baking potatoes in a sieve weighed down with a heavy saucepan over a bowl and allow to drain for 10 minutes.

Put the grated sweet potato and the grated baking potato in a large bowl. Add the rest of the ingredients and stir well.

Transfer into a greased ovenproof dish, approximately 35cm x 20cm.

Cook in the preheated oven for 10 minutes, then turn down the temperature to 180°C/350°F/gas mark 4 and continue cooking for 1 hour.

This is a lovely alternative to serving roast potatoes and it tastes delicious. Also note that it doesn't contain any butter so can be used with meat dishes. Did you know that a South African JP is known as a kugal – 'warm and lovely'?

princess potato salad

serves 10

1kg new potatoes
200g smoked salmon, thinly sliced
300ml sour cream
300g cucumber spears in dill (can be any pickled cucumbers)
1 teaspoon dried dill
salt and pepper to taste

In a large saucepan, boil the potatoes until *al dente*. Drain and leave to one side to cool.

Slice the salmon into small pieces and mix it with the potatoes.

Add the sour cream.

Chop the cucumber into small chunks and mix into the potatoes. Sprinkle them with the dill and season to taste.

Mix everything together thoroughly, transfer to a serving dish and chill before serving.

You might think that this is an odd combination, but it is truly scrumptious. I would serve this dish as part of a Princess buffet.

baked apples

serves 6

5 baking apples, quartered, cores removed
juice of 1 lemon
115g sultanas
40g soft light brown sugar
20g unsalted butter
150ml maple syrup

Preheat the oven to 180°C/350°F/gas mark 4.

Place the apples in an ovenproof dish and squeeze the lemon juice over them.

Add the sultanas.

Scatter the brown sugar over the apples and dot the butter over the top.

Pour on the maple syrup.

Bake in the oven for approximately 30 minutes and serve hot.

A family favourite.

melon, pomegranate and ginger salad

serves 8

2 tablespoons runny honey
110g deseeded pomegranate (you can buy this already prepared, so it's perfect for Princesses)
juice of 1 lemon
1 piece of stem ginger, finely chopped
1 tablespoon stem ginger syrup
2 melons, cut into cubes (use two different types if you like)
mint leaves for decoration

Mix together all the ingredients, apart from the mint leaves, in a serving bowl and refrigerate until ready to serve.

Decorate with the mint leaves.

A fruit salad with all the special ingredients needed for a very sweet New Year.

ginger beer cake: a honey cake alternative

serves 8

175g plain flour
115g caster sugar
1 teaspoon ginger
½ teaspoon cinnamon
115ml ginger beer
55ml vegetable oil
175ml golden syrup
2 eggs
2 teaspoons of dark brown sugar, for decoration

Preheat the oven to 150°C/300°F/gas mark 2.

Beat together all the ingredients, apart from the brown sugar.

Pour the mixture into a greased loaf tin; mine is 23.5cm x 13cm x 7cm.

Sprinkle the brown sugar on the top.

Bake in the preheated oven for approximately 55 minutes, then cool in the tin before turning out and serving.

Similar to traditional honey cake, but I think even more delicious. In fact, it is so wonderful, it's dangerous!

honey biscuits

makes approximately 35

175g softened unsalted butter
100g caster sugar
1 large egg
80g runny honey
250g self-raising flour

Preheat the oven to 180°C/350°F/gas mark 4.

In a mixing bowl, cream the butter and sugar together until pale.

In a separate bowl, lightly whisk the egg.

Add the egg and honey to the butter and sugar mixture and beat until smooth.

Add the flour and beat well until you have a sticky dough.

Place a teaspoonful of mixture onto parchment paper, leaving space for the biscuits to spread (don't worry if they're not perfectly shaped; once they go in the oven, they seem to right themselves).

Bake in the preheated oven for approximately 10 minutes, or until golden.

Remove and leave to cool before removing the biscuits from the paper.

Honey heaven!

jp honey cake: the secret's out!

serves 10

250g self-raising flour
110g soft brown sugar
150ml corn oil
175g golden syrup
75g black treacle
2 large eggs
juice of 1 lemon
1 teaspoon ginger
1 teaspoon mixed spice
1 teaspoon cinnamon
1 teaspoon bicarbonate of soda
150ml boiled water

Preheat the oven to 180°C/350°F/gas mark 4.

Using a mixer, beat all the ingredients, except the boiled water, in a large mixing bowl.

Add the boiled water when the mixture is smooth.

Pour the batter into a 25cm loaf tin.

Bake in the preheated oven for approximately 40–50 minutes.

Turn out and cool before serving.

This recipe is steeped in security, and has been in the family for centuries, so you're very lucky that I've been allowed to tell other JPs about it!

banana, peach and custard cake

serves 8

200g unsalted butter
110g caster sugar
2 large eggs
250g self-raising flour
1 teaspoon vanilla essence
1 banana, sliced thinly
200g tinned peaches, sliced
200g ready-made thick, fresh custard
icing sugar

Preheat the oven to 180°C/350°F/gas mark 4.

In a large mixing bowl, mix the butter, sugar, eggs, flour and vanilla essence together until the mixture is smooth.

Grease an ovenproof dish measuring 30cm x 20cm and put half the mixture over the bottom, spreading evenly.

Place a layer of banana over the mixture, followed by the peaches. Pour the ready-made custard over the fruit.

Put the remaining cake mixture over the custard. This can be quite tricky, but if you use a knife, it helps when you spread it.

Bake in the preheated oven for approximately 30 minutes.

Remove the cake from the oven and leave it to cool. Finally, sprinkle it with fairy dust (icing sugar) before serving.

Try not to eat the custard before you use it for the cake! Oooh, divine!

tarte tatin

serves 6

65g non-dairy margarine
150g caster sugar
9 eating apples, weighing about 850g, peeled and quartered
juice of half a lemon
210g ready-rolled puff pastry

Rub the margarine into the bottom of a heavy-based frying pan. Add the sugar on top, patting it down. In a bowl, squeeze the lemon juice over the apple quarters and mix thoroughly to coat.

Place the apples into the pan in the pattern you eventually want in your tart, (I put them in a clockwise formation) and cook on a low to moderate heat for 50 minutes, carefully turning every 10–15 minutes. The apples should be soft and caramelized.

Preheat the oven to 200°C/400°F/gas mark 6.

Place the ready-rolled pastry onto a floured board. Use your flan dish of choice (mine is 28cm diameter x 4cm depth) as a template and cut round it to form a pastry circle of the correct size.

Slide the cooked apples into the flan dish and then place the pastry on top. Score the top and bake in the preheated oven for approximately 20 minutes. Remove from oven and cool slightly.

While still warm, place the serving dish over the flan dish and turn upside down. Your tarte tatin will drop elegantly onto the serving dish.

A classy tart!

succot
the jewish princess goes camping

Jewish Princes have very many admirable qualities. I'm just trying to think of some... OK, got it: they are *the greatest* dinner guests. When you cook for a Jewish Prince, he will be in raptures – especially if you follow my recipes. Be warned, though: he might compare your food with his mother's culinary skills, either in a good way or a bad way, depending on his mother's cooking.

Every Jewish Prince I know thinks he is a manager of a football team, or at least could be doing a better job than the manager of his favourite football team. Yet for all their *chutzpah*, Jewish Princes are generally brought up in THE JEWISH FAMILY, and therefore suffer with their own particular brand of Jewish Guilt. They can still make excellent husbands – *if* you know how to make them feel guilty *enough*.

However, if we are talking about someone to work the land, put up a shelf or even assemble a piece of flat-pack furniture, DON'T ask a Jewish Prince. This kind of dexterity is not his forte. Which is why, when it comes to the festival of Succot, the Jewish Prince is severely put to the test. Not only does he have to don his outdoor gear (and this isn't a pair of swimming trunks), he needs to be armed with a ladder and a tool-box. While the Jewish Prince probably has these, he might not know where they are. Once found, however, he faces the greatest challenge of all: building a new home called the *Succah* for his family and friends to enjoy.

Oy! And I thought putting up the shelf was a big ask!

Yes, the week-long festival of Succot, otherwise known as The Festival of Tabernacles, requires a *Succah*: a booth-like structure. Even though it is only temporary, it still has to conform to some very strict building regs. These include what height it should be, from what materials it can be built and how the roof must allow visibility to the stars. The word *Succah* means 'booth', and is a reminder of the temporary dwellings lived in by the Jews in their forty years of wandering in the desert following their escape from Egypt.

Obviously, in those days Jewish Princes had a little bit more expertise in the building trade. (I wonder if this is where we got the idea of pyramid selling?)

Anyway, throughout the week of Succot, it is a time to feast and give thanks for the earth's rich bounty and harvest. Invitations to family and friends to share and enjoy eating all meals in the *Succah* are issued, which means we all have to wrap up warm. (Unless, of course, it is raining; then the party moves inside.) To enable the family to sleep (yes, we do this, too) in the *Succah*, it is vital that the *Succah* is sturdy and SAFE.

Think about it: even with all this partying, you don't want to bring the house down.

Dishes reflect the change in season and the mood of harvest festival. Both sweet and savoury dishes are made from fruit and vegetables, plus stuffed foods such as stuffed peppers (see page 94) and *holishkas* (page 88), which is a dish of cabbage and minced beef, plus the 'must-have' dessert for a Jewish Prince (especially mine): apple strudel (page 95).

So, when Succot rolls around very quickly after Yom Kippur, my advice is to make your Jewish Prince my wonderful apple and pine nut strudel and save a piece for the gardener, who I have a feeling might be in the garden with the Jewish Prince's ladder and tool-box, erecting a safe *Succah*, according to the building regulations.

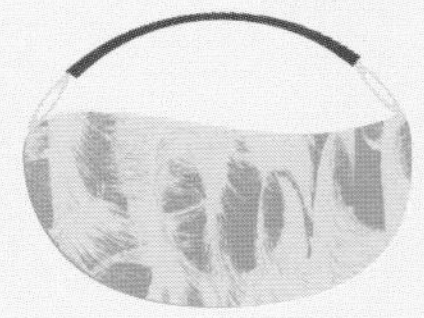

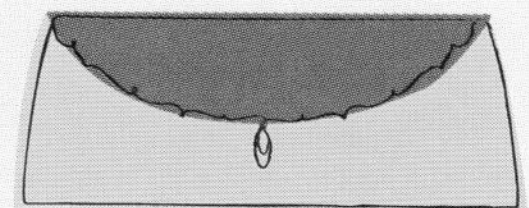

A Jewish Prince asks a Jewish Princess what her favourite fruit is.

'Well,' she says, 'I've always been partial to pairs – of earrings, shoes, handbags...'

challishing holishkas (stuffed meat parcels)

serves 8–10

2 cabbages (fresh, then frozen: see method); Savoy is the easiest
2 tablespoons olive oil for frying
2 onions, diced
1kg minced lamb
200g long-grain rice (dry)
salt and pepper to taste

for the sauce
2 tablespoons gravy granules
500ml boiling water
800ml tomato purée
8 tablespoons brown sugar
juice of 2 lemons
grated rind of 1 lemon

Freeze the cabbages the night before and then take them out of the freezer just before you need them.

Preheat the oven to 170°C/325°F/gas mark 3.

Fry the onions in the olive oil until lightly brown.

Put the cooked onions, mince, rice, salt and pepper in a large bowl and mix together.

Defrost the cabbages slightly, either by pouring hot water over them or in the microwave; this helps separate the leaves easily. You can also place the leaves in a large bowl and cover with boiling water to allow them to be pliable and easy to roll.

Cut out the core of the cabbage with a sharp knife, separate the leaves and wash them.

Take one leaf and place a tablespoon of the mince at the stem end. Roll the leaf around the mince, fold the end over the filling, then fold up the sides to form a long parcel. Place in a large, shallow ovenproof dish, seam-side down.

Continue to make the rest of the cabbage parcels and place tightly next to each other in the dish.

To make the sauce, mix all the sauce ingredients together in a large bowl and pour over the *holishkas*.

Bake in the preheated oven for 2½ hours, making sure you turn the parcels halfway through the cooking time.

This tricky dish, which is traditionally served during Succot, might seem difficult, but if you are challishing *for a* holishka *it is well worth the effort.*

lamb tagine

serves 6–8

4 onions (about 300g), chopped
3 tablespoons olive oil
3 tablespoons hot water
½ teaspoon cinnamon
½ teaspoon turmeric
1 teaspoon dried coriander
½ teaspoon garlic purée
2kg shoulder of lamb
800g tinned tomatoes
1 litre beef or lamb stock
160g dried apricots
160g chopped Medjool dates
100g raisins
2 medium sweet potatoes (approximately 400g)
400g carrots, peeled and chopped
1 tablespoon runny honey
salt and white pepper to taste

Preheat the oven to gas mark 150°C/300°F/gas mark 2.

Now before you Princess Panic at the long list of ingredients, stop, look and listen. Most of these you will find in your store cupboard and it's just a matter of opening jars, tins and bottles, so here we go.

Fry the onions in olive oil until translucent in a large *shissel* or cooking pot: one that's big enough to hold your lamb and fit in your oven.

Mix in the hot water, cinnamon, turmeric, dried coriander and garlic purée. Rub together until it forms a paste, then rub the paste into the lamb.

Brown the lamb in olive oil to seal it all over. Add all the rest of the ingredients and transfer to the preheated oven. Bake for 3 to 4 hours, or until the lamb is tender.

A very simple way of creating this exotic dish.

lemon chilli chops

serves 4

12 lamb chops
salt and black pepper to taste
grated zest and juice of 1 lemon
1½ teaspoon garlic purée
4 stems fresh rosemary
1½ green chilli, chopped finely (use more or less chilli, depending on how hot you like it)
olive oil for frying

Wash the chops and season with salt and black pepper.

Mix all the rest of the ingredients, except the olive oil, and pour over the chops. Leave to marinate for at least 1 hour in the fridge.

Heat a small amount of olive oil in a frying pan – use enough to coat the pan.

Put in the chops and fry, turn over, and cook until the meat is sealed on both sides.

Place under a hot grill and cook until the desired colour, turning them over once during cooking.

If it's hot, barbecue the lot! Serve with a crispy crunchy salad and a chilled glass of wine: lovely!

sweet-and-sour meatballs

makes approximately 45 mini meatballs

for the meatballs
500g minced beef
grated rind of 1 lemon
1 large egg
1 red onion, grated
1 tablespoon mirin
(a sweetened sake or Japanese rice-wine-based sauce)
60g fine matzo meal
a few chilli flakes (optional)
1 tablespoon tomato purée
1 teaspoon dried coriander
1 teaspoon dried parsley
salt and black pepper to taste

for the sauce
800g chopped tinned tomatoes
1 tablespoon tomato purée
2 tablespoons tomato ketchup
227g chopped tinned pineapple in pineapple juice
1 tablespoon caster sugar
1 tablespoon red-wine vinegar
250ml water
1 teaspoon dried parsley
salt and black pepper to taste

Combine all the meatball ingredients in a bowl.

Moisten your hands with water and take a teaspoon of the mixture; shape into a ball. Repeat until all the meatball mixture is used up.

Place all the meatballs in a saucepan of salted water and bring to the boil. Simmer for approximately 40 minutes, then remove the meatballs from the water with a slotted spoon.

To make the sauce, place all the sauce ingredients in a saucepan and simmer for approximately 40 minutes. Check and adjust the seasoning if necessary. If you want a more intense flavour, simply cook it for a little longer; if the sauce becomes a little too thick, add more water.

Add the meatballs to the sauce, combine well and serve. You can prepare this dish early, then simply reheat it.

This dish has so many flavours, it really Princess Perks you up!

princess stuffed vegetarian peppers

serves 8

8 coloured peppers (choose a variety), whole but deseeded, reserving the tops to be used later
2 onions, diced
2 tablespoons olive oil
1 small aubergine, peeled and chopped finely
300g button mushrooms, sliced small
1 teaspoon garlic purée
3 teaspoons of paprika
120g Brie, chopped into small pieces
200g long-grain rice
200ml vegetable stock
salt and black pepper to taste

Preheat the oven to 190°C/375°F/gas mark 5. Place the peppers in an ovenproof dish.

In a large frying pan, fry the onions in the olive oil until transparent, then add the aubergine and mushrooms, followed by the garlic and paprika. Keep stirring the vegetables until they become soft. Transfer to a dish. When cool, stir in the Brie.

Boil the rice with the vegetable stock, according to the packet directions. Drain and cool. Stir in the vegetables and season to taste.

Fill each pepper with the filling and cover each with its reserved top. Bake in the preheated oven for approximately 40 minutes.

A wealth of health!

apple and pine nut strudel

serves 6

330g eating apples
(I use Royal Gala)
100g apricot conserve
50g raisins
50g pine nuts
grated zest and juice of half a
lemon (small lemon)
375g ready-rolled
short-crust pastry
icing sugar to decorate

Preheat the oven to 200°C/400°F/gas mark 6.

Peel and chop the apples and put them into a mixing bowl.

Add the rest of the ingredients, except the pastry and icing sugar, and mix well.

Place the rolled-out pastry on a baking sheet covered with baking parchment.

Spoon the strudel mixture along the centre of the pastry.

Join the ends together to form a strudel, then score the top.

Bake in the preheated oven for 10 minutes, then turn down the heat to 170°C/325°F/gas mark 3 and bake for a further 20 minutes.

Cool, then sprinkle with fairy dust (sieved icing sugar).

A JP twist on the classic apple strudel.

pear and chocolate crumble

serves 6–8

8 pears, peeled and quartered
grated zest and juice of 1 lemon
50g light brown sugar
50ml water
100g dark chocolate, broken into pieces

for the crumble
175g butter or dairy-free margarine, chilled and diced
200g plain flour
100g porridge oats
125g light brown sugar
100g dark chocolate, broken into pieces

Preheat the oven to 170°C/325°F/gas mark 3.

Put the pears, lemon zest and juice, sugar and water into a saucepan over a low heat.

Gently stir the pears from time to time to ensure they are covered by the liquid.

Cook until the pears are tender; this will take approximately 10 minutes.

In an ovenproof dish place the pears, the juice and the broken chocolate pieces.

To make the crumble, rub together the butter and flour, then stir in the rest of the ingredients.

Put this mixture over the top of the pears.

Bake in the preheated oven for approximately 25 minutes.

Serve with ice cream or cream.

A truly lovely combination that everyone adores.

perfect peach cobbler

serves 8–10

6 large peaches, sliced
4 dessertspoons Marsala
170g dairy-free margarine
170g dark brown sugar
170g self-raising flour
2 large eggs

for the topping
8 meringue nests (ready-made)
100g ground almonds
70g flaked almonds

Preheat the oven to 180°C/350°F/gas mark 4.

Put the sliced peaches into a bowl and drizzle with the Marsala. Leave to soak.

Grease a large ovenproof dish – mine is approximately 20cm x 35cm.

Using a mixer, beat together the margarine, sugar, flour and eggs. Spread the mixture on the bottom of the ovenproof dish.

Put the soaked peaches, together with any liquid that has collected, on top of the mixture.

Break the meringue nests into a bowl and blend them with the ground almonds (use a mixer). Blend until the meringue looks like small nuggets. Be careful not to overdo it, though; otherwise it can go to crumbs!

Pour the meringue and almond mix over the peaches.

Scatter the flaked almonds over the meringue topping.

Bake in the preheated oven for 30–40 minutes.

Serve immediately.

This is best eaten as soon as it is made; otherwise the liquid can make the meringue soggy if it is left to stand for too long.

strudel biscuits

makes approximately 80

for the dough
450g plain flour
250g unsalted butter
175g caster sugar
2 large eggs

for the filling
6 tablespoons (approximately) seedless raspberry jam
450g mixed chopped dried fruit
1½ teaspoons cinnamon
6 teaspoons cocoa powder
3 teaspoons caster sugar

for the topping
1 egg
1½ teaspoons cinnamon mixed with 3 teaspoons of caster sugar
icing sugar for decoration

Preheat the oven to 180°C/350°F/gas mark 4.

Mix together the flour, butter, caster sugar and eggs until a dough is formed. Divide the dough into three pieces.

Take one section and roll it out on a floured tea towel. (Do not use a ridged tea towel as you will get grooves in the dough!) Your pastry should be approximately 40cm in length and 25cm in width, and about 5mm thick.

Spread a thin layer of jam (roughly two tablespoons) over the dough.

Dust half a teaspoon of cinnamon over the jam.

Sprinkle 150g of mixed fruit over the jam and cinnamon.

Dust the fruit with two teaspoons of cocoa powder.

Line a baking sheet with baking parchment.

Take the ends of the tea towel and roll up the pastry into a Swiss roll shape, then transfer the strudel onto the baking sheet. If you feel the strudel is too big to transfer, cut it in half.

Brush some beaten egg over the dough.

Mix one teaspoon of caster sugar with half a teaspoon of cinnamon and sprinkle over the egg wash.

Repeat this procedure twice more using the reserved dough.

Use a sharp knife and cut the strudel at an angle three-quarters of the way down. Repeat every 2cm the length of the strudel.

Bake for 20 minutes in the preheated oven.

Remove from the oven and cut the biscuits through along the indentations.

Dredge with icing sugar.

Once you've got the hang of these, they're not as daunting as you think. I was even surprised that fussy Junior Princesses adored them!

chanukkah

the festival of lights

Whatever age you may be – or, if you're a Jewish Princess, whatever age you may *admit* to being – Chanukkah (or Hanukkah, Hanukah or Chanukah, depending on where you're from) holds the magic key that unlocks the child in all of us. This eight-day-long festival is filled with songs; my all-time favourite is *Moaz Tzur yeshu'ati:* 'The Cat's in the Cupboard and You Can't Catch Me'. There is the symbolic lighting of the *menorah*, the nine-branched candelabra that marks each of the eight nights – one head candle known as the *Shamas* lights all the others. Then there are the indulgent fried foods that are eaten and, of course, did I mention, the Princess Presents that are exchanged?

It really is a festival of miracles. First, the story of Chanukkah centres on Judah Maccabee, who led his army to win a great victory over the Syrians. Why is this a miracle? Jewish men are not particularly known for their warrior-like skills – well, not in my house, anyway. After the battle was won, the Maccabees entered the temple in Jerusalem and completely cleaned it from to top to toe, removing all idols and re-dedicating it to G-d, (the word *Chanukkah* means 're-dedication'). Once again, this is indeed a miracle: I can't even get my lot to clean the bathroom sink!

To re-dedicate the temple, sacred oil was used to light the eternal flame. Unfortunately, they only had enough oil for one night, but miraculously it lasted for eight, so every year it is marked and celebrated with the Festival of Lights, otherwise known as Chanukkah.

Now, because I am The Jewish Princess, I want to talk about the Princess Presents and the fabulous food that is eaten over this holiday – and did I mention the Princess Presents?

It really is another miracle if you don't put on weight during this festival. After all, what can be more delicious than to feast on fried foods? From potato pancakes known as *latkes* (page 110) dipped into apple sauce, sour cream or even tomato ketchup, to mouth-watering doughnuts of any flavour (try my Cheater's Doughnuts on page 112), not to mention carefully unwrapping the chocolate money that is traditionally given, nibbling around the sides and then letting the centre melt in your mouth...

Well. I did tell you this festival unlocks the child in all of us.

With regard to presents, some families just give money, known as Chanukkah *gelt*. Fine by me. Others create a Chanukkah chest (but relax: this doesn't entail a trip to the plastic surgeon) and give a small gift every night. You know what they say: 'All good things come in small packages' – especially if they are from Bond Street. Sometimes gifts are only given to children. However, as I said before and will say again:

Chanukkah UNLOCKS THE CHILD IN ALL OF US!

So as you read this chapter, think of it as a Princess Present from me to you. I bet it will take a miracle for you not to get in the kitchen and start frying TONIGHT!

How does The Jewish Princess
celebrate the Festival of Lights?

She phones the hairdresser
and books a full set!

corn fritters

makes approximately 20

200g self-raising flour
1 teaspoon baking powder
2 large eggs
150ml full-fat milk
1 teaspoon dried parsley
2 x 260g (drained weight) tins sweet corn
salt and black pepper to taste
vegetable oil (for frying)

Beat together all the ingredients except the oil. Be sure to season the mixture well.

Fill a deep-sided frying pan at least a third full with the oil.

Take a tablespoon of the mixture and drop it into the hot oil. You can do about six at a time, depending how big your frying pan is.

Fry the fritters until golden brown, then turn over to do the other side.

Leave to dry on kitchen paper, to absorb the oil, before serving.

A great way for Junior JP's to eat their vegetables. This also makes a great change from potatoes.

feta fatter potatoes

serves as many as you wish

allow 2 small potatoes cut
into quarters (wedge style)
for each person
olive oil
1 teaspoon dried oregano
per portion
salt to taste
3 tablespoons good
mayonnaise per portion
20g feta cheese per portion

Preheat the oven to 200°C/400°F/gas mark 6.

Put the potatoes in a roasting tin, cover them with the olive oil and sprinkle with the dried oregano.

Season with salt.

Roast for approximately 40 minutes, or until golden.

Mix in the mayonnaise and the crumbled feta cheese to serve.

Fabulous, and well worth getting fatter for!

mini maccabiah balls

makes approximately 45

1kg potatoes
2 leeks, white part only
2 tablespoons olive oil
salt and pepper to taste
2 large eggs, beaten
plain flour
corn oil for frying

Peel the potatoes and boil them until soft. Mash the potatoes and leave to cool.

Cut the leeks into small pieces.

Put the two tablespoons of olive oil in a saucepan and fry the leeks until soft. Add the leeks to the mashed potatoes and season.

Heat some corn oil in a frying pan.

Take a teaspoon of mixture and, after moistening your hands with water, roll it into a ball. Repeat with the rest of the mixture.

Dip the balls in the beaten egg, then roll them in the flour.

Drop them, a few at a time, into the hot oil and fry until golden brown.

When removing from the oil, place the balls on a kitchen towel to drain.

Delicious served hot – and they also make great canapés.

princess tahini fried chicken

serves 4–6

1 medium chicken, skinned and cut into 8 pieces
2 heaped tablespoons tahini
100g plain flour
2 teaspoons smoked paprika
1 teaspoon dried parsley
salt to taste
vegetable oil

Preheat the oven to 180°C/350°F/gas mark 4.

Rub the tahini into the chicken so that it has a 'massage' all over.

Put the flour, paprika and parsley into a plastic bag, add each piece of chicken and shake well to coat.

Season with a little salt.

In a deep frying pan, heat enough vegetable oil to cover the chicken pieces and fry each piece until pale golden.

Remove and place on kitchen paper to absorb any excess oil.

Transfer to a baking dish and bake in the oven for approximately 45 minutes. Remove and serve.

This is KKFC: the Kosher King of Fried Chicken.

sweet potato and apple latkes

makes approximately 40

2kg sweet potatoes, peeled
3 eating apples, peeled
2 onions, peeled
4 large eggs
300g plain flour
salt and black pepper to taste
vegetable oil

In a food processor, grate the sweet potatoes, apples and onions finely, then mix in the rest of the ingredients thoroughly and blend until smooth.

In a deep frying pan, heat enough vegetable oil to cover the *latkes*.

Take a tablespoon of mixture and use your hands to form it into a flat patty. Repeat using the rest of the mixture.

Fry the *latkes* in the oil until golden brown.

Latkes *with a JP twist that would also be fabulous to serve during Rosh Hashanah (see page 62).*

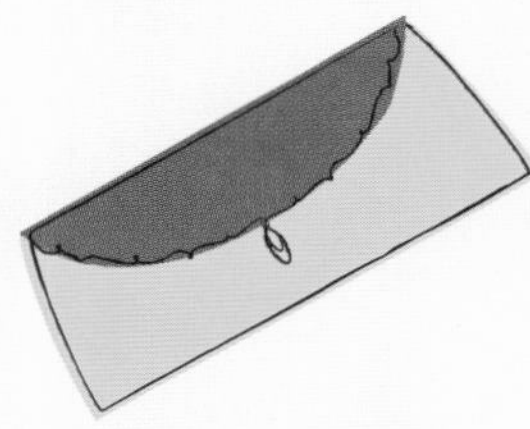

zucchini, italian-style

serves 8

4 courgettes
400g plain flour
7 eggs
700ml corn oil
salt to taste

Top and tail the courgettes.

Slice them in half, then cut each half into 6 slices lengthways.

Put the flour in a shallow dish.

Beat the eggs and put them in another shallow dish.

Heat the corn oil in a large frying pan.

Take a piece of courgette and cover it with flour, then dip in egg and then in the flour again. Repeat this method for the rest of the courgette pieces.

Fry the courgettes in oil until golden brown.

Remove with a slotted spoon and place on kitchen paper to absorb any excess oil. Add seasoning to taste, then serve.

An Italian on the side that doesn't pinch your bottom. SHAME!

chanukkah cheaters' doughnuts

makes approximately 34

1 large *challah*, crusts removed and broken into small pieces
2 large eggs
500ml unsweetened soya milk
1 teaspoon baking powder
vegetable oil for frying
caster sugar

Mix all the ingredients, except for the caster sugar and the vegetable oil, in a large bowl.

Once the liquid has soaked into the *challah*, hand-blend the mixture until smooth.

Heat the vegetable oil in a wok.

Drop a dessertspoon of the mixture into the oil and fry the doughnut until it is golden on each side.

Remove with a slotted spoon and place on kitchen paper to absorb any excess oil.

Roll the doughnuts in the sugar while they are still warm.

A fantastic alternative to doughnuts that can be served any time, even for dessert with fruit on the side just to make them seem a little healthier!

chocolate cherry fudge

makes approximately 60 pieces

405ml condensed milk
100g caster sugar
60g softened unsalted butter
100g dark chocolate
100g milk chocolate
60g glacé cherries

Put the condensed milk, sugar and butter into a non-stick saucepan. Heat, stirring constantly over a medium heat until the butter melts.

Lift and lower on the heat as necessary, but continue cooking and stirring until the condensed-milk mixture thickens and turns a pale golden colour.

In a separate double saucepan (bain-marie), or using a small heatproof bowl placed over a saucepan of simmering water, melt the chocolate over a low heat.

Mix the chocolate into the golden toffee mixture, then add the finely chopped glacé cherries.

Grease and line an oblong tin (roughly 23cm x 30cm) with parchment paper.

Pour the fudge into the tin and smooth over with a damp spatula to get a nice even top surface. Refrigerate.

When ready to serve, cut into small squares and EAT!

Fudge-y, yummy, scrummy and not *good for the bummy!*

chocolate truffles

makes approximately 40

200g dark chocolate
 (70% cocoa solids or more,
 depending on taste)
8 tablespoons double cream
1 teaspoon Cointreau
 (or liqueur of choice)
40g icing sugar
1 teaspoon cocoa or cinnamon

Gently melt the chocolate in a double saucepan (bain-marie) over a low heat, or use a small heatproof bowl placed over a saucepan of simmering water. Remove from the heat, leave to cool slightly, then stir in the double cream and liqueur.

When cool, pour the mixture onto a piece of parchment paper and refrigerate for approximately 10 minutes.

Place another piece of parchment paper over a chopping board (I stick the parchment paper down so that it doesn't move).

Put the mixture by half-teaspoons onto the parchment paper. Refrigerate for a couple of hours.

Place the icing sugar and cocoa (or cinnamon) in a plastic bag, add the truffles and shake until the truffles are well covered.

Remove them from the bag. Place on your serving dish and leave in the fridge until you are ready to dive in.

Intense chocolate. Intense training the next day!

holiday fruit cake

serves 10

500g mixed dried fruit
4 tablespoons Scotch whisky
225g dark brown sugar
225g unsalted butter
2 large eggs
225g self-raising flour
1 teaspoon mixed spice
100ml full-fat milk
icing sugar (optional)

Put the mixed fruit in a bowl and pour the whisky over the fruit. Cover with plastic wrap and leave to stand for 24 hours.

Preheat the oven to 180°C/350°F/gas mark 4.

Put the rest of the ingredients into a mixer and blend until you have a smooth consistency.

Add the boozy fruit and mix well.

Grease a 24cm round cake tin. Pour in the cake mixture.

Bake in the preheated oven for 45 minutes, then remove and allow to cool before serving.

When ready to serve, sprinkle with icing sugar, if desired.

A Princess tribute to Uncle Eddie.

hot chocolate pudding

serves 8

for the pudding
4 medium eggs, separated
300ml semi-skimmed milk
5 heaped tablespoons cocoa powder
175g caster sugar
175g softened unsalted butter
175g self-raising flour
1 teaspoon baking powder

for the icing
115g icing sugar
2 tablespoons hot water

Whisk the egg whites until stiff.

In a saucepan, heat the milk and cocoa together, stirring until you have a smooth paste. When the cocoa mixture has come to the boil, switch off the heat. Stir in the egg yolks one at a time, then add the caster sugar.

Put the butter, flour, baking powder and the cocoa mixture in a bowl and use a mixer to whisk until smooth. Fold in the egg whites.

Grease a heat- and microwave-proof bowl 21cm diameter x 14cm depth. Pour in the mixture, put it in a microwave and heat on high for 10–11 minutes.

While the pudding cooks, stir the icing sugar and water together in a saucepan until it is smooth. Turn out the pudding and glaze with the icing.

You will be immediately transported back to a school chocolate-pudding moment!

toffee nuts

serves 6–8

a pinch of salt
150g almonds
100g pecans
100g macadamia nuts
100ml water
4 tablespoons caster sugar

Grind or sprinkle the salt over the nuts.

Put the water and sugar into a frying pan and fry the nuts until all the water has absorbed and the nuts are sticky.

Great served hot over ice cream.

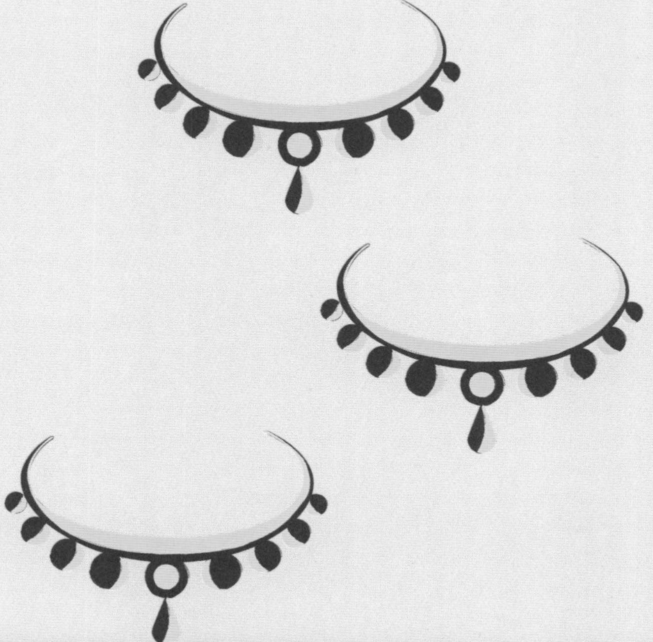

2

celebrations

the bris brunch

Once a Jewish Princess has got over the joy of giving birth to a boy – this could take a lifetime; I mean, you have to cope with the amazement that a Princess can actually produce a human who has different bits from her own – the inevitable Princess Problem of changing the nappy begins. Has this happened to anyone else? I hear it can be quite good for the skin... The next realization is that a Princess must prepare for the *bris*: the circumcision. Eight days after the birth, if all goes well and your baby boy is in perfect health, your house will be full of people watching a man tackle your son's tackle.

The *bris* (Yiddish) or *brit* (Hebrew) is every Jewish Princess's nightmare. Your son will cry, you will cry (I recommend waterproof mascara), your mother will cry, your father will cry – *everyone* will cry. Now I know it is supposed to be a time of great joy and celebration when your son makes his covenant with G-d, (*brit* is the Hebrew word for 'covenant') and is the most important commandment in the Torah, but truth be told, we are dealing with a protective Jewish mother, who will not let a fly hurt her new son, never mind an axe-wielding doctor.

OK, so I'm getting a little hysterical here with the axe part, but you know what I mean.

The *mitzvah* ('good deed') is that the *bris* should be carried out by the father – *if* he is qualified to do the job. (Mine has trouble putting up a shelf.) However, if not, this role is handed over to a *mohel*. For a Jewish Princess, only a top-class surgeon will do: a sort of royal *mohel*.

The *bris* ceremony is traditionally performed early in the morning and is a very formal occasion, the most important religious event in a Jewish boy's life. It really is a two-for-one, because as part of the ceremony, your heir is given his Hebrew name. A strict etiquette has to be followed, and members of your family are given different honours.

Your *bubbeleh*, dressed for the occasion in a designer nightie (for easy access), is placed on a special Princess Pillow. A Princess Pal who hasn't yet been blessed with children, known as *kvtarin* (g-dmother), hands the precious bundle to her hubby, the *kvater* (g-dfather). He continues the baby pass-the-parcel to your seated father-in-law, who has the greatest honour of all acting as the *baal brit* 'master of the circumcision ceremony' or *sandek* (Greek for g-dfather), who holds your offspring for the duration.

The actual circumcision is over very quickly; however, your mother and mother-in-law might have nail marks in their arms from where you have been clinging on. Then, as with any Jewish get-together, even in the case of a circumcision, food becomes a very important part of the day.

A brunch is served – but with NO SAUSAGES!

What did the Jewish Princess
say to her baby?

'Gucci, Gucci, Gucci!'

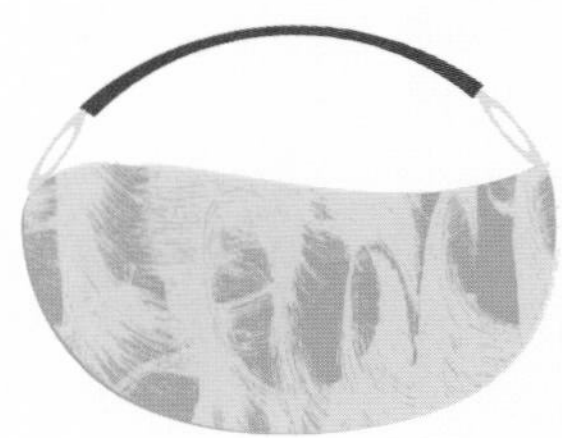

bagel chips

makes approximately 16

4 bagels a couple of days old (any flavour)
100ml olive oil
salt to taste
½ teaspoon cajun spice
½ teaspoon dried chives

Preheat the oven to 180°C/350°F/gas mark 4.

Very carefully cut the bagels horizontally into 4 or 5 very thin rings.

Mix the olive oil, salt, cajun spice and chives together in a bowl.

Brush each side of the bagel rings, place them on a baking sheet, then bake for 40 minutes, turning them over halfway through cooking.

This is a great way of using up old bagels to make a delicious crunchy bite that can be used at any meal. I love serving them at lunch with a variety of dips and crudités, but they can even be served with drinks before dinner. Why not experiment with grated cheese, flavoured oils and other herbs – whatever takes your fancy? Store in an airtight container.

a collection of cream cheeses

sun-dried tomato and basil cream cheese

serves approximately 20

400g light cream cheese
5 sun-dried tomatoes in extra-virgin olive oil, chopped
6 basil leaves, chopped
salt and black pepper to taste

Use a hand-blender to mix all the ingredients together except the salt and black pepper.

Season to taste and refrigerate until ready to serve.

Dip, spread, even have it on a bagel for a breakfast in bed (now wouldn't that be Princess Perfect?).

tuna and celery cream cheese

185g tinned tuna, drained
100g full-fat cream cheese
2 sticks of celery, finely chopped
1 shallot, finely diced
100g cucumber, cubed
salt and pepper to taste

Mix all of the ingredients together in a large mixing bowl, then refrigerate until ready to serve.

Delicious on toast or in a baked potato – mmmm.

avocado and spring onion cream cheese

4 spring onions, finely chopped (use the white part only)
1 large ripe avocado
400g light cream cheese
½ teaspoon paprika
salt to taste

Use a hand-blender to mix all the ingredients together. Refrigerate until ready to serve.

A 'wicked' green cream cheese that is good for the skin!

smoked salmon and cream cheese

200g smoked salmon, sliced into slivers
300g cream cheese
juice of half a lemon
1 tablespoon of full-fat milk
black pepper to taste

Mix all of the ingredients together in a large mixing bowl, then refrigerate until ready to serve.

The Princess Perfect accompaniment to the bagel.

tortilla princess-style

serves 6

50ml olive oil
1 tin new potatoes in water, drained weight 345g, thinly sliced
1 large onion, peeled and sliced
8 large eggs
salt and black pepper to taste

Heat the oil in a frying pan. Add the potatoes and onions to the pan and cook slowly. (This takes a while).

When the onions are translucent and the potatoes are slightly brown, remove from the frying pan and pat dry with kitchen towel to remove excess oil. Reserve any oil left in the frying pan for later.

In a bowl, beat the eggs with the salt and paper, then add the potatoes and onions. Leave to rest for 10 minutes (this doesn't mean going to lie down on your bed, though...).

Turn the grill on your oven to high.

Reheat the oil in the frying pan and pour in the egg mixture.

Try to layer the potatoes in the frying pan; the smaller the frying pan, the thicker the tortilla. Leave to cook on a low heat.

When the bottom of the tortilla has set, run a knife around the edge to prevent it from sticking to the sides of the pan, then place the frying pan under the hot grill for a couple of minutes to finish cooking.

When it has cooled slightly, turn the tortilla out onto a serving dish.

It's better served at room temperature. When serving, slice into triangular sections or, if serving with drinks, cut it into small squares pronged with cocktail sticks.

For something extra-special, why not drape a thin slice of smoked salmon over the tortilla and add a dollop of crème fraîche on the side? Don't forget the Champagne!

shakshuka: egg and tomato

serves 6

2 tablespoons olive oil
2 onions, diced
2 red peppers, cut into thin strips
3 tins chopped tomatoes;
 total weight 1.2kg
1 teaspoon dried cumin
1½ teaspoon garlic purée
1 teaspoon paprika
1 tablespoon tomato purée
1 tablespoon caster sugar
salt and black pepper to taste
6 large eggs

In a large, deep frying pan, fry the onions in the olive oil until translucent. Add the peppers and continue frying until they are soft.

Stir in the tomatoes, cumin, garlic purée, paprika, tomato purée, sugar, salt and pepper and simmer for 30 minutes. The mixture will thicken.

With the back of a ladle, make six small indentations in the sauce and break the eggs into them.

Cover the frying pan with a lid and continue to cook for approximately 4 minutes, depending on how you like your eggs.

Take the frying pan off the heat and bring to the table to serve.

Shakshuka *means 'all mixed-up', and I know a few family members this applies to first thing in the morning...*

muesli breakfast cookies

makes approximately 40

100g chopped dates
100g chopped dried figs
100g walnuts
100g oats
100g self-raising flour
½ teaspoon ginger
½ teaspoon cinnamon
2 eggs
1 teaspoon baking powder
100g caster sugar
20g olive oil

Preheat the oven to 170°C/325°F/gas mark 3.

Put all the ingredients into a bowl and beat with a food mixer until the mixture comes together.

Moisten your hands with water and roll the dough into small balls.

Line a baking tray with parchment paper, add the dough balls and bake in the preheated oven for approximately 25 minutes, or until golden brown.

Cool before serving.

Breakfast bites that will keep you going until elevenses – when you will be ready for a cup of coffee and another muesli cookie.

breakfast banana loaf

serves 6–8

120g wholemeal flour
1 teaspoon baking powder
1 large egg
2 medium ripe bananas
100g mixed dried fruit and nuts
120ml clear honey
80g softened unsalted butter

Preheat the oven 170°C/325°F/gas mark 3.

Beat all the ingredients together in a large bowl.

Pour into a greased loaf tin (mine is 21cm x 12cm) and bake for 30–35 minutes.

Turn out onto a wire rack and leave to cool.

A yummy way to start the day.

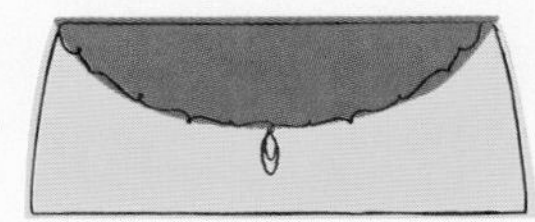

cinnamon cake

serves 10

250g unsalted butter
280g caster sugar
2 large eggs
400g self-raising flour
300ml full-fat milk
25g cinnamon (a small pot)

for the topping
175g walnuts
160g light brown sugar
60g cubed unsalted butter

Preheat the oven to 180°C/350°F/gas mark 4.

Beat together the butter, sugar, eggs, self-raising flour, milk and cinnamon.

Spread the mixture evenly in a 24cm loose-bottomed cake tin.

To make the topping, break the nuts first by placing them in a sandwich bag and bashing them with a rolling pin.

Put the broken nuts in a mixer together with the sugar and butter.

Mix until it resembles crumbs, but be careful not to overdo it – keep an eye on this process.

Sprinkle this over the cake mixture and bake in the preheated oven for approximately 60–75 minutes.

Be sinful: have a slice of cinnamon cake with butter.

chocolate rugelach

makes approximately 20

for the pastry
150g softened unsalted butter
150g full-fat cream cheese
150g sour cream
75g caster sugar
300g plain flour
½ teaspoon cinnamon
½ teaspoon baking powder

for the filling
2 tablespoons cocoa
2 tablespoons caster sugar

1 beaten egg for egg wash
icing sugar for decoration

Beat the butter and cream cheese together in a bowl until smooth. Add the sour cream and blend well.

Sieve together the dry ingredients and add them to the mixture. Beat until the mixture becomes a soft, sticky dough.

Divide the dough into 2 balls and refrigerate for 2 hours.

Preheat the oven to 180°C/350°F/gas mark 4.

Remove 1 ball. On a very well-floured board, knead the dough for 1 minute

Still checking that the board is constantly well-floured, roll out the dough into a large circle approximately 40cm in diameter and 1mm thick (don't be too fussy).

Once this is done, divide it into 10 pieces (like a pizza), then sieve over 1 tablespoon of cocoa powder and sprinkle on 1 tablespoon of caster sugar.

Take each section and roll it from the outside in, then shape into a crescent (croissant-like) shape.

Repeat the same exercise for the second ball of dough.

Place the *rugelach* on a baking sheet lined with parchment paper and bake for approximately 20 minutes.

When cool sprinkle with fairy dust, a.k.a. icing sugar.

The Jewish pain au chocolat.

The bar mitzvah

One day a Jewish Princess will wake up with her heart racing, in a sweat, knowing there is something she has to do – but what? Don't Princess Panic. This isn't a 'mature moment'; you haven't reached old ladydom just yet. It is simply the realization that your son's or daughter's bar or bat mitzvah is just TWO years away! Which is why now is the time to open the bar mitzvah file and start preparing for this very special event.

Why do we Princesses Panic? Well, a bar/bat mitzvah is a very difficult function to organize. It is celebrated when a boy turns thirteen and when a girl turns twelve, (well, we Princesses are always a little more advanced than our male counterparts, wouldn't you say?) At this special time, the child becomes a 'son or daughter of the commandments' (this is actually what bar or bat mitzvah means) and takes the first steps into adulthood. This event is a very, very big deal in a Jewish family's calendar of events – and you need a very big deal to pay for it.

It is so easy to get caught up completely in the whole 'bar mitzvah bubble'. And if you're not careful, this event can take on a life of its own. Like your son (or daughter), it grows quickly from an idea to a representation of everything you have achieved and everything you wish and hope for in your son (or daughter's) future.

So as your son opens his books to study his portion of the Jewish law, to *lein* (sing) or chant, depending on his voice (every Jewish mother hopes her son will have the voice of Pavarotti, the looks of Brad Pitt and the intelligence of Einstein), or your daughter works on her *dvar Torah*, a speech relating to her week's Torah portion (every mother hopes her daughter will marry a boy who has the voice of Pavarotti, the looks of Brad Pitt and the intelligence of Einstein), you can work out how many work-outs it will take so that when you walk into the celebratory party, wave to your guests, dance to that bar mitzvah classic 'Reach for the Stars' in the mother of all mother-of-the-bar-mitzvah outfits, you will know there won't be even so much as a hint of the commonly known (and dreaded) 'bar mitzvah bat wing'.

Two years will fly by. You will become an expert in everything from chocolate fountains to life-size ice sculptures – all of which will stand you in good stead for future events, such as your daughter's wedding.

So in this chapter, please don't think I expect you to cater your son or daughter's bar/bat mitzvah; you have enough to do, what with hair, nails and outfit-hunting. However, I have created 13 delicious recipes for you or your Princess Pals to make when you get together at the traditional pre-bar/bat mitzvah lunch to discuss that very important topic:

What *are* you going to wear?!

A Jewish Princess
is a Jewish Princess
all her life.

A Jewish Prince
is a Jewish Prince
until he marries a wife.

spinach dip

serves 8

160g chopped spinach leaves
200g mozzarella cheese, grated
150g Cheddar cheese, grated
200ml crème fraîche
250ml single cream
½ teaspoon grated nutmeg
1 tablespoon Parmesan cheese, grated
tortilla chips

Preheat the oven to 180°C/350°F/gas mark 4.

Put the spinach leaves in a saucepan over a low heat and keep stirring until the leaves have wilted.

Add the mozzarella, Cheddar, crème fraîche, single cream and nutmeg. Stir until all the cheese has melted.

Pour the mixture into an ovenproof dish.

Sprinkle with the Parmesan and bake in the oven for 10 minutes.

Serve the dip hot, with tortilla crisps on the side.

Dip and quip.

hummus

serves 8

225g drained and washed chickpeas (you can buy them in water; 1 tin weighs about 410g)
100ml olive oil
2 teaspoons garlic purée
100g tahini
juice of 3 small lemons
2 tablespoons sheep milk yoghurt
salt and black pepper to taste
2 pinches of ground ginger

Place all your ingredients in a food processor.

Blend until the mixture forms a smooth paste.

Check the seasoning, adjust if necessary, and serve.

To start or to dip with slices of hot pitta bread.

easy aubergine pâté

serves 8

3 onions, diced
6 tablespoons olive oil
2 teaspoons garlic purée
2 aubergines (roughly 800g), cut into small pieces
salt and black pepper to taste
juice of half a lemon
3 tablespoons tahini
1 handful fresh chopped coriander
3 tablespoons double cream

Fry the onions in 3 tablespoons of the olive oil and add the garlic purée. When soft, add the aubergines and the remainder of the oil.

Add the salt (you will need quite a bit) and black pepper.

Stir-fry until the aubergines are cooked. Remove from the heat.

Add the lemon juice, tahini and coriander and blend with a hand blender.

When cool, add the double cream and check the seasoning; adjust it if necessary.

Serve cold.

An auber-genius recipe.

pear waldorf salad

serves 8

14 celery sticks, 'de-stringed' and chopped
3 pears (I use Conference), chopped
120g walnut halves
6 Medjool dates, chopped
1 orange, segmented, plus the juice of half an orange
3 tablespoons mayonnaise

Mix all ingredients together in a bowl and serve.

A JP twist on the original.

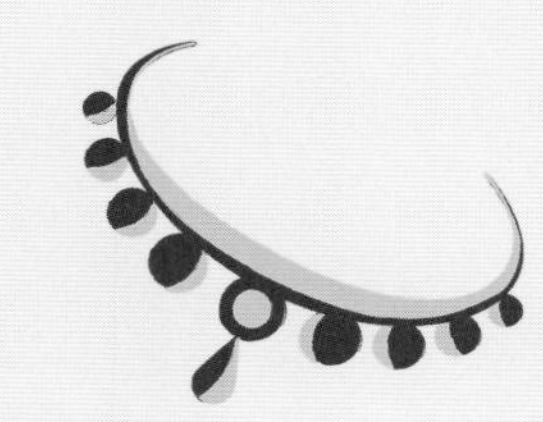

endemame and noodle salad

serves 6–8

500g frozen shelled endemame beans
4 spring onions, sliced
4 tablespoons sesame oil
1 teaspoon soy sauce
400g cooked egg noodles
1 bunch fresh coriander (approximately 100g), finely chopped
sea salt and black pepper to taste

From frozen, put the endemame beans in boiling salted water, bring them back to the boil, then drain.

Fry the spring onions in the sesame oil and soy sauce. Fry for a couple of minutes, until they are *al dente*.

Combine the endemame beans, spring onions, all the leftover oil, cooked egg noodles and chopped coriander, and add the sea salt and black pepper. Mix well, then serve.

This is delicious served warm. Endemame beans are very trendy and don't have to be eaten only in Japanese restaurants.

coleslaw – hold the mayo

serves 6

for the salad
1 cabbage, shredded
175g sultanas
3 spring onions, finely chopped (use only the white part)

for the dressing
50ml olive oil
30ml white-wine vinegar
1 tablespoon lime juice
2 tablespoons runny honey

Mix all the salad ingredients in a large bowl.

Mix the dressing ingredients thoroughly and pour over the salad.

Transfer into the bowl you are going to serve it in – and serve.

No mayo makes this Princess Perfect for a low-fat lunch.

sugar-snap peas, spinach and chilli salad

serves 6

for the salad
400g sugar-snap peas
110g spinach leaves
8 baby tomatoes, diced

for the dressing
1 red chilli, deseeded and finely chopped
a good squeeze of fresh lemon juice
a slug of virgin olive oil
salt and black pepper to taste

Chop the sugar-snap peas, spinach leaves and tomatoes and place in a bowl.

To make the dressing, place all ingredients in a small bowl, mix well, dress the salad and serve.

I haven't put specific amounts for the dressing, as it is up to each Princess to decide how spicy she would like her salad.

roasted butternut squash and red onion salad

serves 8

3 butternut squashes, total weight roughly 2kg
3 white onions, sliced thinly
2 red onions, sliced thinly
3 tablespoons olive oil
grated Parmesan

for the dressing
juice and grated rind of 1 lemon
1 tablespoon light brown sugar

Preheat the oven to 200°C/400°F/gas mark 6.

Wash the butternut squash and bake them whole in the preheated oven for approximately 25 minutes. Remove and leave to cool.

When cool, peel, remove the seeds and cut the squash into small cubes, approximately 3cm square.

Put the onions and squash on baking parchment which has been placed on an ovenproof tray and drizzle with the olive oil.

Turn down the heat to 190°C/350°F/gas mark 5 and bake for 25 minutes. Leave to cool.

Mix the dressing ingredients together, pour over the squash and add the Parmesan.

Partially cooking the squash saves all that bother of trying to cut and peel this tough customer, so it's Perfect for Princesses.

challah pizza

serves 4–6

1 *challah* (or *challah* rolls); use a *challah* that is a couple of days old
ready-made pasta sauce

for the topping
200g feta cheese (or cheese of choice)
basil leaves (approximately 15)
any other toppings you desire

Cut the *challah* lengthwise through the middle (the same if you are using *challah* rolls).

Spread with the sauce.

Add cubed feta and any other topping of your choice.

Decorate with the basil leaves.

Put under a hot grill and cook until the cheese browns, approximately 5 minutes. Serve immediately.

Be imaginative. If you don't like feta, substitute it with another cheese: mozzarella, etc. Be creative and use a variety of different toppings: anchovies, tinned artichoke and sweetcorn… whatever takes your fancy for a Princess Perfect Pizza! If you want to make these into canapés, just buy mini challah *rolls.*

mozzarella and onion flan

serves 4

2 medium onions, sliced
2 tablespoons olive oil
500g ready-made shortcrust pastry
2 tablespoons red-onion chutney (or chutney of choice)
salt and black pepper to taste
1 dessertspoon dried basil
1 large egg, beaten
125g mini mozzarella balls (approximately 16)

Preheat the oven to 190°C/175°F/gas mark 5.

Sauté the onions in the olive oil.

Roll out the pastry on a floured board and line a 26cm flan dish.

Stir the red-onion chutney into the sautéed onions and season to taste with the salt and pepper.

Spread the mixture over the pastry and scatter with the dried basil.

Bake in the preheated oven for 20 minutes.

Remove from oven, add the beaten egg and dot around the mozzarella cheese.

Bake for a further 10 minutes. Cool slightly, then serve.

Looks fabuloso!

asparagus borekas (pastry puffs)

serves 6

375g ready-rolled puff pastry (if you can't find ready-rolled, just roll out your own and make a large rectangle)
150g black pepper cream cheese if unavailable, mix black pepper into regular cream cheese)
12 medium-size asparagus spears
1 large egg, beaten
1 handful of sesame seeds

Preheat the oven to 180°C/350°F/gas mark 4. Place the pastry on a floured pastry board or chopping board. Spread the cream cheese evenly over the pastry.

Put the trimmed asparagus spears in a saucepan and cover with water. Boil for approximately 1 minute until they are *al dente*. Remove with a slotted spoon and dry with kitchen paper.

Take two asparagus spears and place them on the edge of the pastry, one on top of the other. Roll into a cigar shape. Trim the excess pastry with a sharp knife and use a fork to indent the ends. Score the top of the *boreka* in three places. Continue until all the asparagus spears and pastry are used up. Mix the sesame seeds with the beaten egg and brush this on top of the pastries.

Bake in the preheated oven for 30 minutes; during the last 5 minutes turn the *borekas* over to ensure even cooking. To serve, cut in half and stack at angles. Serve hot or cold.

If you don't like the filling suggestion, try cooked mushrooms, onions, pesto, cheese and tomato… whatever your Princess pleasure.

mushroom bake

serves 6

2 red onions, chopped
3 tablespoons olive oil
750g mixed mushrooms of your choice, sliced
salt and black pepper to taste
2 teaspoon garlic purée
1 teaspoon dried oregano
2 handfuls chopped basil leaves
1 handful of tarragon
250g mascarpone
125g ricotta
200g Emmental, grated
400g penne pasta (cooked *al dente*)
180g goat cheese (rind removed)

Preheat the oven to 180°C/350°F/gas mark 4. Grease a large ovenproof dish.

Fry the onions in the olive oil until they are soft. Add the mushrooms, seasoning, garlic purée and herbs. Cook until the mushrooms are soft.

Stir in the mascarpone and ricotta, turn off the heat, then stir in the Emmental. Add the cooked pasta and mix well.

Place in ovenproof dish and dot goat cheese over the top.

Bake in the preheated oven for 20 minutes, or until you can see that the mixture is bubbling and the cheese has melted.

You won't have 'mush room' for anything else after this delicious dish!

princess rabbit

serves 6

375g ready-made puff pastry
4 large eggs
3 tomatoes, sliced
150g grated Cheddar cheese
(or choose your own flavour)
salt and black pepper to taste

Preheat the oven to 190°C/375°F/gas mark 5.

Roll out the pastry onto a floured glass board into a rectangular shape approximately 1.5cm thick. Place on a baking tray lined with parchment paper. Pinch the sides with your fingers (take off your rings!) to form a ridge all the way round.

Break the eggs, one by one, into each quarter of the pastry.

Add the tomatoes and grated cheese so that they are scattered evenly.

Season with salt and black pepper.

Bake in the preheated oven for approximately 20 minutes, or until cooked and golden.

Nosh on this while you have a good old rabbit.

The Jewish Princess
wanted to be the first to hold
a bar mitzvah in space.

Her only worry
was that it might
lack atmosphere.

the wedding

the princess and the prince

When I was a child, my favourite fairy tale was *Cinderella*. I think it was the glass slippers I was attracted to. (Even in my formative years I was VERY interested in shoes.) I was so captivated by this tale that I would spend hours with my nose stuck in a Disney compilation, reading and re-reading, dreaming and pondering when, how and where I would meet my Prince Charming and that most important question:

What would he look like?

So when did I meet Prince Charming? Well, like all fairy tales, sit comfortably and I'll begin...

Once upon a time, I was dragged to a charity event to make up the numbers, (not quite a ball, more of a cocktail party). I looked across a crowded room and saw a Prince who I thought was very handsome. I asked to be introduced, which was not my usual Princess-like behaviour, but he had amazing eyes. My heart skipped a beat, but did he have eyes only for me? Did we dance until midnight? Was I wearing a pair of extraordinary shoes? No, no and YES (well, I *am* a Jewish Princess.) He was there with another Princess.

DRAT! This story is not getting off to the best start.

So, are you wondering already, does my fairy tale have a happy ending? Well, hold on a minute; this Princess had some work to do.

We became pals and dating began. He set me up with all HIS friends (this is getting worse) and every week I trudged out on blind dates, dressed for success (of course), but was tucked up in my bed before midnight – ALONE.

Well, just what sort of Princess do you think I *am*?

So time passed and Prince Charming was still seeing other Princesses (*OY VEY!*) and phoning to arrange dates for me with his friends. Did this Princess despair or give up? NEVER! But if this fairy tale was going to have a happy ending, I knew that I would have to use all my powers of Princess Persuasion and steer him in the right direction.

I was used to getting my own way.

So I took drastic action and asked Prince Charming for his hand in marriage – ONLY JOKING! Actually, I asked him to accompany me to a ball (my Princess Pal was getting married). He accepted. He happened to be free that night.

He turned up *late* (some things never change). Can't we get anything in this fairy tale right? YES, we danced the night away. YES, I was wearing a beautiful ball gown. YES, I had on fabulous shoes and YES, he was finally beguiled by my charm! By midnight, Prince Charming and I were an 'item' and he asked for my hand in marriage.

Well, not quite.

It did take two months, but then he proposed in his own unique way:

'I will be speaking to your father on Friday.'

Did I accept?

I wasn't even sure if he had proposed.

So like all wonderful fairy tales, let's cut to the wedding scene. It isn't necessary to get bogged down in the finer details, such as how do you keep two families happy, where are you going to live and how are you going to afford to EAT? Let's move swiftly on and with one flick of my magic pink pen get to the fun part: THE DRESS, THE DRESS AND THE SHOES!

Picture the scene: a warm summer's day, (finally, something is going to plan). The stunningly beautiful Princess (it's getting better by the minute) has been bedecked in the bridal room; Jewish tradition dictates that Prince Charming has a look at his bride before the ceremony, just to check he is marrying the right Princess and not the older uglier sister, as in the case of the biblical story of Jacob, Leah and Rachel.

The Princess has walked (well, tottered) down the aisle to the sounds of a 'Neil Diamondesque' *chasen* (singer) and an angelic choir, in her very high-heeled glass-ish slippers. There's an audible gasp from the congregation at her amazing, AMAZING dress (are you surprised?) and train (all six feet of it). She is followed by a procession of bridesmaids and page boys, all suitably (beautifully) dressed. She has released her arm from her father's vice-like grip and has circled her Prince seven times, to symbolize the protective care she will wrap him up in (she's never letting him out of her sight again) and that all barriers between her and Prince Charming are now waved aside (it's his lucky night).

After the seventh circle, she feels dizzy and exhausted (a sign of things to come), but this tradition has finally been completed – and let me tell you, it isn't easy with six feet of train.

She stands under a forest of flowers that adorn the *chuppah*, (the wedding canopy) representing the home or PALACE (please G-d) that the Prince and Princess will build together. Her mother and future mother-in-law are looking fabulous in their dresses that DON'T clash (I told you I get my own way) on one side of the *chuppah* and her father and father-in-law are looking grand on the other.

The *erusin* (betrothal blessings) and the *ketubah* (the marriage contract) have been read and the Prince has promised that he will love, honour and provide (he better) for his Princess according to Jewish law (the Princess stays *shtoom*!). The Prince and Princess have sipped the blessed wine. The rabbi has given his words of advice and told the Princess's father to 'shut up' and stop sobbing; after all, he is not losing a Princess, but gaining a Prince (who can now pick up her shopping bills and boy, are they heavy!).

After a small hiccup (literally), the Princess waits for her new life to begin.

It is now the duty of the Prince to complete the ceremony by stamping on and breaking the wrapped glass. This is to remind the couple of the destruction of the Temple of Jerusalem, and that they must not neglect their moral obligations. She looks down, hoping he will succeed first time, otherwise their marriage might be cursed, and notices that he is wearing the most beautiful, BEAUTIFUL pair of Gucci evening shoes. At that moment, as the glass breaks, the photographer goes into a frenzy, the choir breaks into a rendition of 'Sunrise, Sunset' and *Mazel tov*! rings out around the synagogue. The Princess knows that they are, like a pair of Jimmy Choos, the perfect fit and, like all wonderful fairy tales, they will live happily ever after.

THE END

Well, not quite.

In the Jewish Princess fairy-tale wedding, food plays a very important part (of course). Before the bride has even been whisked off in her carriage from her parents' palace to the synagogue, the Princess bride's mother invites friends and family by royal appointment to *shlep naches*, wish her dolly *mazel tov* and to see THE wedding dress. When the guests arrive, a table is heaving under a weight of goodies to welcome them. This is traditionally known as 'The Table', and it is filled with miniature sandwiches and petite sweet treats.

So in this chapter I have used my Princess Powers and as your fairy godmother I have waved my magic Pink Wand to create food fit for a royal 'Table'.

May you all live happily ever after!

As she watched her
husband stamp on the
glass under the *chuppah,*
the Jewish Princess
knew that
this was the last time
he would ever put
his foot down.

how to create a jp sandwich selection

I have been busy designing my own range of Princess Sandwiches. Not only do they taste fabulous, but of course, being designer, they look absolutely scrumptious. However, every Princess has different (but still elegant) tastes, so if you don't fancy the fillings I've suggested in this section, why not experiment? With so many delicious deli options the list is endless.

Whatever fillings you choose, here are a few Princess sandwich pointers to help you create the perfect sandwich selection:

* Always remember to take your butter out of the fridge so that it is soft and ready to use.

* Invest in an electric bread knife.

* When the sandwiches are ready but the guests have not yet arrived, to keep your sandwich Princess Perfect, take some kitchen paper and dampen it, or use a dampened tea towel, then lay it over the top of your sandwich selection to keep them moist.

* If you need extra sandwiches, just double the quantities I have given, depending on how many guests you have invited.

* When serving, use your designer touch and make these little bites as pretty as a Princess Picture. Give them space to shine: less is more and there will be requests for repeat orders, trust me.

the handbag sandwich

makes 10

10 slices of brown bread
unsalted butter, softened
280g smoked salmon
black pepper to taste
1 lemon

With a 9cm cookie cutter, cut a circle from each slice of bread. Spread each circle with a thin layer of butter.

Cut a lemon in half (half for lemon juice, half for decoration).

Place approximately 14g of smoked salmon on the bread and drizzle with a little lemon juice and black pepper.

Fold the sandwich into a half-moon shape.

Take a pair of kitchen scissors and snip off any overhanging smoked salmon.

Add a very thin slice of lemon, also in a half-moon shape, allowing it to poke out of the sandwich to create the 'handle' of your 'handbag'.

A Princess creation that is so elegant to eat. Of course, in true Princess style, one handbag is never enough…

triple deckers

makes approximately 20

for the egg mayonnaise
4 large hard-boiled eggs, shelled
30g unsalted butter, melted
1 heaped tablespoon mayonnaise
pinch of paprika
salt to taste

for the triple deckers
unsalted butter, softened, for spreading
20 slices of dark wholemeal bread
10 slices of white bread
10 cherry tomatoes, each cut into three thin slices
a handful of watercress

Mash together all the egg mayonnaise ingredients in a mixing bowl.

Remove all crusts from the bread. Spread a thin layer of butter on all the bread slices.

To make your Triple Decker, place a slice of wholemeal bread on the bottom and spread with the egg mayonnaise, then place the white bread on top, butter-side up. Next, add the tomatoes and watercress, and finally add another piece of wholemeal bread, butter-side down.

Cut into four elegant fingers (rather like mine).

Once, twice, three times a winner.

princess pinwheels

makes approximately 60

10 slices of white bread
unsalted butter, softened
130g cream cheese
black pepper to taste
20 thin asparagus spears; use a 250g tin (drained)

Take a sharp bread knife (I use an electric carving knife) and remove all the crusts from the bread.

Spread each slice of bread with a thin layer of butter.

Spread a thin layer of cream cheese on each slice. Season to taste with the black pepper.

Place two asparagus spears near the edge of each slice of bread. Roll each slice of bread tightly to form a cigar shape.

Wrap tightly in cling film and pack close together to keep the cigar shape.

Refrigerate for a minimum of 2 hours; however, they can be stored overnight.

When ready to serve, remove the cling film from the cigar shape and slice widthways into six, forming little round sandwiches and thus creating the Perfect Princess pinwheel.

Fancy, shmancy!

kosher wine kichels

makes approximately 60

300g plain flour
250g butter (unsalted), softened
150ml kiddush wine
(or sweet red wine)
1 pinch salt
1 large egg
1 teaspoon vanilla essence
150g caster sugar
2 tablespoon icing sugar

for decoration
half a glacé cherry per biscuit

Preheat the oven to 170°C/325°F/gas mark 3.

Beat together all ingredients except the glacé cherries and icing sugar.

Using 2 teaspoons, spoon out the mixture onto sheets of baking parchment.

Decorate with the glacé cherries.

Bake for 10–12 minutes, or until golden brown.

When they come out of the oven, dust with icing sugar and leave to cool.

Store in an airtight container.

I know glacé cherries are a little tacky, but to give this kichel *an authentic feel, just think retro!*

blueberry and sour cream sponge cake

serves 8

250g unsalted butter
250g light brown sugar
2 large eggs
250g self-raising flour
1 teaspoon vanilla essence
3 tablespoons sour cream
4 egg whites
150g blueberries

Preheat the oven to 180°C/350°F/gas mark 4.

Mix all ingredients together except the egg whites and blueberries to form a batter.

Whisk the egg whites until stiff and fold them into the mixture. Stir in the blueberries.

Pour the batter into a greased 20cm cake tin and bake in the preheated oven for 40 minutes.

This is a great way of getting those nutritious blueberry vitamins into your system. They are youth in-juicing!!

florentines

makes approximately 21

175g corn flakes
250g dried fruit-and-nut mix (if you can buy fruit-and-nut mix with chocolate drops, this is even better)
85g glacé cherries
1 x 397ml tin condensed milk
3 sheets edible rice paper
100g plain chocolate

Preheat the oven to 180°C/350°F/gas mark 4.

Put the corn flakes in a food mixer or blender until they have broken up (this should take only a few seconds), then add the fruit-and-nut mix, glacé cherries and condensed milk.

Mix together.

Put the rice paper on a baking tray. Take a heaped tablespoon of the mixture and place on the rice paper. Keep doing this with the rest of the mixture, leaving a small space in between the florentines.

Bake in the preheated oven for 10 minutes.

Remove from the oven and leave to cool on a wire rack.

Break the individual florentines off the main sheet of rice paper. (You will see that the remaining rice paper underneath each florentine holds the biscuit together.)

Break the chocolate into smaller pieces and put it in a double saucepan (bain-marie), or use a heatproof bowl over a saucepan of simmering water. Melt slowly.

Use a spatula to coat the bottom of the florentines in chocolate.

Leave to dry chocolate-side up.

Whenever you bake these, make sure you have guests coming; otherwise you will eat them all yourself as they are so amazing.

princess scones

makes approximately 14

450g self-raising flour
55g unsalted butter
2 teaspoons baking powder
60g caster sugar
½ teaspoon salt
60g sultanas
200ml full-fat milk

Preheat the oven to 180°C/350°F/gas mark 4.

Mix the above ingredients together, leaving the milk until last. When you add the milk, do it slowly, and if you see the mixture coming together, you may not need to use all the milk.

Flour a glass board and place the dough on it. Cover a rolling pin lightly with flour and roll out the dough. The thicker the dough, the bigger the scone will be.

Use a large, round cookie cutter to cut out the first scone. Continue to do so with the rest of the dough.

Place the scones on a silicone baking sheet and bake in the preheated oven for at least 10 minutes, or until the tops go slightly brown.

Serve hot or cold with butter, strawberry jam and if you want to be naughty, full-fat cream, whipped… mmmmmmmm!

I promise these will all be scone very quickly.

triple chocolate chip cookies

makes approximately 36

120g brown demerara sugar
120g caster sugar
2 large eggs
150g softened butter, cubed
1 teaspoon vanilla essence
¼ teaspoon salt
500g self-raising flour
200g chocolate of choice
(I use a combination of white, dark and milk chocolate; you can even use Smarties or Buttons)
1 tablespoon milk
icing sugar for dredging

Preheat the oven to 180°C/350°F/gas mark 4.

Beat the sugars and eggs together slowly. When the mixture has turned paler, add the butter piece by piece.

Add the vanilla essence, salt, self-raising flour and mix well. Break the chocolate into small pieces and add it to the mixture. Add the milk and beat. By now the mixture should look like a soft dough.

Lay out some parchment paper on a baking sheet. Using your hands, roll the dough into small balls (approximately a dessertspoonful for each) and place on the paper. Flatten each ball slightly with the back of a spoon. The cookies will spread slightly, so allow enough room between each.

Bake in the preheated oven for 10–12 minutes. Dredge with icing sugar when still warm. Cool before serving.

Mmmmmmmmmmmmmmmmm with a glass of milk!

3
feasts

hosting the designer dinner party

When I give a dinner party, my aim is to be the 'hostess with the mostess'. To do this, my friends, family and, most importantly, I (well, I *am* the hostess) need to *enjoy* it. After all, if I'm going to do all that shopping and cooking, I really want to get the 'mostess' out of it. So when I throw a dinner party, of course I want to make it a Designer Dinner Party. I realized many years ago that Princesses just love coming over to my home to spend time away from theirs. They do not expect a 'menu' when they sit down to eat; they do not expect a Michelin-starred chef in the kitchen. In fact, if you were that good, they would never reciprocate because they would be just too intimidated.

When you're in the kitchen creating, my advice is to find your own *signature style* – create a look that works for you. To do this, you may go through many different phases, but as all great designers know, there is nothing wrong with experimentation. After all, when you let your creative juices flow, you can come up with some culinary masterpieces. I admit that I've made mistakes along the way (just don't tell anyone), and that sometimes my food does not make the grade and has been cut (or thrown out) from my designer dish list. However, when Princess Perfected, my designer dishes look *haute* – but take note: they definitely are not.

When you think of fashion (a Jewish Princess does a lot of this), styles never really go away for good; they're just re-invented and come back in a slightly different guise. What you wouldn't consider wearing one season is top of your list the following year (skinny-leg jeans, for example). It's the same for a dinner party: one season a pudding is *passé* and the next it is the height of 'kitsch-in' and back on the dish wish list.

To get you started, then, on the following pages you'll find some more of my top tips for hosting a successful Designer Dinner Party.

* Think about who you are going to invite. Your guests don't need to know each other, but the right mix of personalities makes a great cocktail.

* Make sure you are aware of any Food Fears or dietary requirements your guests might have. If you have a veggie, don't get edgy; I've included a delicious vegetarian feast on page 194.

* Write a list of what you are cooking and leave it somewhere you can see it so you won't forget anything.

* When deciding what to make, go for something you feel secure with. Remember, most people like plain, simple cooking and actually do not like rich, heavy sauces (hooray!).

* You can always buy in part of the meal. A lot of my Princess Pals leave out the starter and just serve more canapés, or even opt for a sensational sushi platter (purchased from a sensational sushi chef). I think this is a terrific idea, as it allows more time for everyone to relax (and maybe drink a little more of the pink stuff than they normally would – and yes, OK, I *am* talking about myself). However, if you enjoy good things in small packages (what JP doesn't?), then try making a selection of goodies from my canapé collection on page 174.

* Before your guests arrive, go through a mental check-list – something along the lines of the following:

1. Flowers arranged.
2. Candles lit.
3. Music on.
4. Pink stuff in the fridge.
5. Downstairs loo is clean, plenty of toilet paper and clean hand towel.

6. Spray rooms with a delicious perfume.
7. Food is cooking; check the oven is actually on and at the correct temperature.
8. Leave time to look gorgeous: you don't want to greet your guests in your bath robe. Or maybe you do. Who am I to judge?
9. Dress to impress, but make sure you don't *shvitz*.
10. If you wear killer heels, make sure that they are *comfy* killer heels (they do exist)!

* When it comes to desserts, it's simply unnecessary to recreate a dessert trolley of choices. I just make one that is naughty (all the Princesses say, 'NO', but eat it anyway) and always have another that is a fruity finale. Surprisingly, the fresh fruit is always most popular with the men. To make too many desserts spells stress – literally, it does: DESSERTS spelled backwards is STRESSED – so beware. It is not *how many* desserts you make, but how delicious they are. I know I've done a good job if, after the first spoonful goes into a mouth, the eyes close, the chin tilts back and there's a pause before 'Mmmmm.' This makes me a happy hostess.

Of course the end of a dinner party is just as important as the beginning, so I always serve a plate of Princess Perfect chocolates. Even though my Princess Pals cry out, 'Oh, no: I'm full', it's amazing how their hands creep across the table to find that delectable treat. I gather my flavoured teas, fill up the cafetière (marvellous wedding present), choose my mint leaves and everyone sips and quips until it is time to leave.

So if you use the menu plans I have provided in this chapter, when the doorbell rings, smile, because you know what you have been designed to do:

HAVE A GOOD TIME!

a collection of canapés

green olive tapenade

4–5 slices of toast make approximately 20

163g pitted green olives
grated peel of half a lemon
1 teaspoon chopped fresh coriander
½ teaspoon caster sugar
½ teaspoon olive oil
salt and pepper to taste
4–5 slices, total, of brown and white bread

Use a blender or food processor to blend the olives until a rough mixture forms.

Add the rest of the ingredients, except the bread, and mix well, then place in the fridge.

Toast the white and brown bread and slice into small squares.

Put a portion of the tapenade on top and serve.

A can't-go-wrong canapé.

blinis

makes approximately 42

180g buckwheat flour
300ml unsweetened soya milk
1 egg
¼ teaspoon salt
2 grinds of black pepper
1 teaspoon baking powder
1 tablespoon vegetable oil

Beat together all the ingredients, except the vegetable oil, until you have a thick, creamy batter.

Heat the vegetable oil in a frying pan. When hot, pour away any excess.

Drop in a dessertspoon of batter for each blini and fry.
As they dry and bubble, turn over and fry the other side.
This takes very little time.

Leave to cool.

When ready to serve, top with smoked salmon, a sliver of lemon and chopped chives or chopped fresh dill; sour cream, cream cheese or any other topping – just use your imagination.

These look so impressive your guests will think you have had the caterer in (stay shtoom!*).*

pizza straws

makes approximately 26

375g ready-rolled puff pastry
4 tablespoons passata
1 teaspoon garlic purée
salt and black pepper to taste
100g black olives, sliced

Preheat the oven to 200°C/400°F/gas mark 6.

Line a baking tray with parchment paper.

Put the rolled out pastry on the baking tray.

Mix together the passata, garlic purée, and salt and black pepper.

With a spatula, spread a very thin layer of the tomato mixture over the pastry.

Sprinkle evenly with black olives.

With a knife, mark down the middle and then into straws, roughly 3cm wide.

Bake for approximately 15 minutes, or until golden. Use a pizza cutter to divide them. Serve warm.

A straw to adore!

a chicken dinner party

loaded avocados

serves 8

2 hard-boiled eggs, grated
1 red pepper, finely diced
half a cucumber, finely diced
salt and black pepper to taste
2 tablespoons olive oil
1 tablespoon red-wine vinegar
2 teaspoons garlic purée
8 small avocados

Put the eggs, chopped pepper and cucumber into a bowl. Season to taste with the salt and pepper.

Mix together the olive oil, red-wine vinegar and garlic purée. Pour it over the egg mixture.

Cut one avocado in half, discard the stone, and place the avocado half on a serving dish.

Spoon the filling into each avocado half. They're supposed to be 'loaded', so don't worry if the dressing spills out.

Be careful when you remove the avocado stone with a sharp knife; you don't want to end up in bandages when you greet your guests!

stuffed chicken thighs

serves 8

garlic-infused olive oil
4 shallots, chopped
20 button mushrooms, sliced
16 cherry tomatoes
a few slices of red chilli
4 handfuls of fresh spinach leaves
16 chicken thighs, skinned and boned out
salt and black pepper to taste

Preheat the oven to 180°C/350°F/gas mark 4.

In a frying pan, heat a small splash of the garlic-infused olive oil. Fry the shallots. When they soften, add the mushrooms, tomatoes and chilli. Season to taste with a little salt and black pepper.

When these soften add the spinach – the leaves will wilt in seconds. Add a little more salt and black pepper if desired.

Wash and season the chicken. Lay the pieces out flat in a large casserole or ovenproof dish. Put the cooked ingredients in the centre of each thigh and fold the other half of the thigh over them.

Add a little garlic-infused olive oil to the bottom and top of each piece of chicken.

Put in the oven and cook, uncovered, for approximately 25 minutes.

This smells delicious as it cooks. A healthy and mouth-watering meal that is so quick and looks incredibly impressive – like a hot dinner date, (not that I would know...).

noo potatoes!

serves 8

24 new potatoes
120g black olives, sliced
1 red pepper, sliced
1 green pepper, sliced
6 vine tomatoes, halved
olive oil
balsamic vinegar
2 garlic cloves, chopped
salt and black pepper to taste

Preheat the oven to 180°C/350°F/gas mark 4.

Allow 3 potatoes per person.

Wash the potatoes and place them in a roasting dish.

Add the olives, peppers and tomatoes. Cover with olive oil and a splash of balsamic vinegar, and sprinkle over the chopped garlic.

Season to taste.

Bake for 1 hour and 15 minutes, or until the potatoes are cooked.

These potatoes are perfect for a dinner party: so colourful and they have a perfect Mediterranean feel.

sesame sugar-snap and asparagus crunch

serves 8

240g asparagus
300g sugar-snaps peas
2 tablespoons sesame oil
1 tablespoon teriyaki sauce
1 tablespoon sesame seeds
salt and black pepper to taste

Wash the asparagus spears and the sugar-snap peas.

Remove the end of the asparagus spears and cut them in half.

In a wok, heat the sesame oil. Add the teriyaki sauce, sesame seeds, salt and black pepper to taste.

Stir-fry the vegetables for a couple of minute, then test the crunch. Serve immediately.

Crunch-eliscious!

cauliflower with a kick

serves 8

1 cauliflower (roughly 600g), cut into small florets
2 tablespoons olive oil
1 onion, finely diced
200g cherry tomatoes
½ teaspoon turmeric
½ teaspoon garam masala
1 large pinch of caster sugar
salt and black pepper to taste

Cook the cauliflower in boiling salty water until it is *al dente*.

Drain off the water and remove the cauliflower.

Fry the diced onion in the olive oil until translucent.

Add the rest of the ingredients and the cauliflower and fry until soft. Keep turning to prevent the cauliflower from catching.

Check the seasoning and adjust it if necessary before serving.

A colourful way of serving cauliflower that looks great on the Princess plate! You can also make this earlier in the day and just reheat.

almond pudding

serves 8

6 large eggs
200g caster sugar
1 teaspoon almond essence
175g ground almonds
30g flaked almonds

Preheat the oven to 170°C/325°F/gas mark 3.

Separate the eggs. Whisk the egg whites until stiff.

In a separate bowl, beat the egg yolks, sugar and almond essence together until pale.

Once pale, slowly add the ground almonds.

Next, slowly add the egg whites.

Line a 24cm square (depth 6cm) tin with parchment paper, pour in the mixture and scatter the flaked almonds over the top.

Bake for approximately 30 minutes. Cool slightly before serving.

Can be served hot or cold. The taste is almond heaven.

clementines in caramel

serves 4

10 clementines
400g caster sugar
water to cover the clementines
200ml orange juice
1 tablespoon of brandy

Remove all peel from the clementines and leave the fruit whole. Put in a heatproof glass dish ready for serving.

Put the caster sugar in a saucepan and add enough water just to cover it – about 400ml. Bring to the boil for 10 minutes, until the sugar starts to caramelize (you can stir a little), then turn down and simmer for a further 20 minutes, or until it has turned light brown in colour.

Take the saucepan off the boil and slowly add the juice. Bring the saucepan back to the boil and stir the caramel with a wooden spoon. Be careful, as it might froth up at this stage. This will take approximately another 10 minutes.

Just before you are going to take the saucepan off the heat, add the brandy.

Pour the caramel over the clementines and place in the fridge.

After a couple of hours turn the fruit over to ensure that you get a good coverage of caramel. Serve when desired.

This dessert is fat-free, so help yourself to two darling clementines!

a fish dinner party

mushroom soup

serves 8

6 shallots, chopped
3 tablespoons olive oil
900g white cup mushrooms
2 tablespoons vegetable
stock powder
1.125 litres water
1 teaspoon dried oregano
1 teaspoon dried sage
1 bunch chopped flat-leaf parsley
2 dessertspoons kiddush wine
salt and black pepper to taste
300ml double cream

Fry the shallots in the olive oil.

When they are soft, add the mushrooms and fry until soft.

Add the rest of the ingredients, except the cream.

Bring to the boil and simmer for 20 minutes.

Blend well.

Stir in the cream and check the seasoning; adjust if necessary before serving.

Serve with a sprig of thyme.

halibut kebabs

serves as many as you like

ingredients per kebab

¼ red onion
1 white cup mushroom
allow 100g skinned halibut fillet, cubed, per person (1 fillet will make 4 cubes)
2 chunky pieces of courgette
1 chunky piece of yellow pepper
2 mini asparagus
fresh thyme
salt and black pepper to taste
basil-infused olive oil

Preheat the oven to 180°C/350°F/gas mark 4.

Take a wooden kebab stick and thread a piece of onion on one end and a mushroom on the other. Whatever you want to do in the middle is up to you, but after each piece of fish, tie thyme around the kebab stick.

When you have loaded up the kebab stick (it will look very pretty), season to taste.

Lay on a baking sheet covered with parchment paper.

Drizzle with the basil-infused olive oil.

Bake for approximately 15 minutes, turning halfway through.

Colourful and crunchy – and a healthy fish kebab.

brill basmati rice

serves 8

2 tablespoons olive oil
1 onion, peeled
300g basmati rice
600ml boiled water
salt to taste

Put the oil in a saucepan and put the onion in the middle.

Gently warm the oil and let the onion disperse its flavours for just a minute – do not let the onion burn.

Put the rice in a sieve and wash with water until the water runs clear.

Put the rinsed rice into the saucepan that has the onion in. Pour in the boiled water. Season to taste.

Mix together and bring to the boil, then place on a low heat.

Put a sheet of foil over the saucepan and cover tightly. Place the lid on top of the foil. Simmer for half an hour, then turn off the heat and leave for 10 minutes.

Break the onion into the rice.

Check the seasoning and adjust if needed before serving.

Rice that is soooo nice!

oy ya broccoli

serves 8

800g broccoli florets
grated rind of 1 large lemon
1 squeeze of lemon juice
2 tablespoons garlic-infused olive oil
salt and black pepper to taste

Put the broccoli in boiling salted water for a few minutes, so that it is still undercooked. Drain.

Heat the olive oil in a frying pan and fry the broccoli, for approximately 1 minute (depending on how you like your broccoli), with a squeeze of lemon juice and the lemon rind.

Season to taste and serve.

A tasty way of serving broccoli that keeps the freshness and colour locked in.

ratatouille princess-style

serves 8–10

6 tablespoons light olive oil
1 red onion, cut into chunks
3 courgettes, approximately 600g
2 small aubergines, approximately 500g
2 red peppers, sliced
12 small santini tomatoes, approximately 150g
1 tablespoon fresh thyme
20g parsley (curly leaf), chopped
1 garlic clove
salt and pepper to taste
140g tomato purée
1 tablespoon caster sugar

Heat the olive oil in a deep saucepan.

Add the chopped onion and fry until translucent.

Top and tail the courgettes and cut each into three sections. Slice each section in half lengthwise and then thinly slice (approximately 5cm in length). Put in the saucepan.

Slice the aubergine into thick slices and then slice again several times. Add to the other ingredients, together with the sliced pepper.

Add all the rest of the ingredients into the saucepan.

Put a lid on the saucepan and turn down the temperature. Cook for approximately 30 minutes, stirring occasionally.

This wonderful array of colours makes you wish you were in France, where this dish originates. Ooh la la!

dark chocolate and limoncello mousse

serves 8

200g dark chocolate
(70 percent cocoa solids)
20g non-dairy margarine (or butter)
4 large eggs, separated
60g sieved icing sugar
4 teaspoons limoncello
(Italian lemon liqueur)

Melt the chocolate using a double saucepan (bain-marie) or a heatproof bowl over a saucepan full of simmering water. When it has nearly melted, add the margarine and stir until the mixture has melted.

Remove the chocolate from the heat and leave to cool for a few minutes, then carefully add the egg yolks one at a time.

Beat the egg whites until stiff.

Add the sieved icing sugar to the chocolate mixture.

Fold in the egg whites and then add the limoncello.

Pour into a serving dish or individual coffee cups, and refrigerate until ready to serve.

This soft, velvety chocolate mousse has an amazing, refreshing taste. Limoncello is from Italy; if you can't get it where you live, may I suggest that you hop on a plane and pick up a bottle?

pear tart

serves 8

375g ready-rolled puff pastry
200g pear purée (ready-made)
about 10 Rochas pears (380g), peeled and sliced
2 tablespoons light brown sugar
1 teaspoon cinnamon

Preheat the oven to 200°C/400°F/gas mark 6.

On parchment paper, lay out the pastry and pinch a ridge all the way round.

Smooth on a thin layer of pear purée.

Place the pear slices on top of the purée. Don't worry about making it too perfect: rustic is 'the look' wanted here.

Sprinkle with the sugar and cinnamon.

Put in the preheated oven and cook for approximately 25 minutes.

So easy and looks very St Tropez: très délicieux!

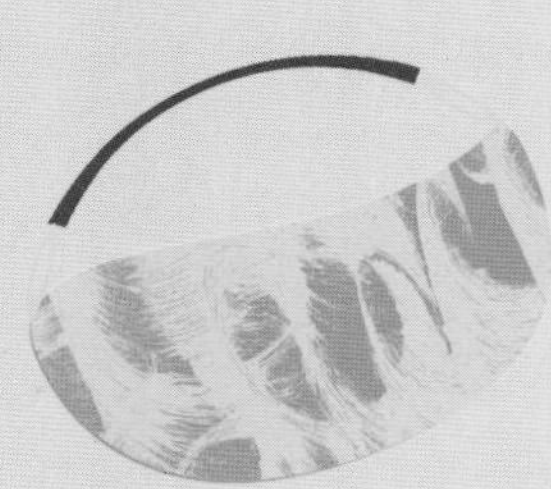

vegetarian princess, italian-style

minestrone

serves 8

2 onions, diced
1 garlic clove, chopped
3 tablespoons olive oil
260g potatoes, peeled and chopped
6 tomatoes, skinned (to remove the skin, pop the tomatoes in boiling water, cover, leave for a couple of minutes and the skin peels away)
half a cauliflower, cut into small rosettes
3 celery sticks, peeled and chopped
2 courgettes, peeled and chopped
4 carrots, peeled and chopped
200g green beans, topped and tailed, then cut in half
4 bay leaves
2 teaspoons herbes de provence
1 sprig rosemary
1 x 260g tin haricot beans, rinsed
approximately 3 litres vegetable stock, or enough stock to cover the vegetables
salt and black pepper to taste

Fry the onions and garlic in the olive oil until soft.

Add all the rest of the ingredients. Bring to the boil.

Simmer for approximately 30 minutes, or until the vegetables are soft.

Serve with Parmesan and crusty bread. One bowl is never enough!

vegetable lasagne

serves 8

for the lasagne
3 onions, diced
2 aubergines, chopped
10 tablespoons olive oil
1 tablespoon garlic purée
salt and black pepper to taste
20g butter
250g spinach leaves, washed
250g mascarpone cheese
110g grated Cheddar cheese
¼ teaspoon ground nutmeg
300g fresh lasagne sheets

for the topping
25g butter
75g mascarpone cheese
110g Cheddar cheese, grated
salt and black pepper to taste

Fry the onions and aubergines in the olive oil and garlic purée until soft. Season well.

Add the butter and the spinach and cook until the spinach wilts; this takes less than a minute.

Switch off the heat and stir in the mascarpone, Cheddar and nutmeg.

Check the seasoning and adjust it if necessary.

Grease an ovenproof dish (27cm x 27cm).

In a separate saucepan, cook the fresh pasta with a dash of olive oil and salt for 2 minutes, until *al dente.*

Spoon a thin layer of sauce in the bottom of the dish, then create a layer of pasta and so forth until you have used all the sauce and there is a layer of pasta at the top.

Preheat the oven to 180°C/ 350°F/gas mark 4.

To make the topping, stir the butter and mascarpone cheese together in a saucepan until it turns into a liquid. Season to taste.

Pour this on top of the lasagne and sprinkle the Cheddar cheese over the top.

Bake in the preheated oven for 20 to 25 minutes, or until the cheese is golden.

A lazy lasagne.

melting nutty raspberry meringue cake

serves 8 (or 6 with very big appetites!)

5 egg whites
300g caster sugar
1 teaspoon vanilla essence
150g hazelnuts, bashed to resemble breadcrumbs
284ml double cream
450g fresh raspberries
icing sugar to taste

Preheat the oven to 160°C/325°F/gas mark 3.

Whisk the egg whites until stiff. Slowly add the caster sugar. Fold in the vanilla essence and hazelnuts.

Line 2 x 25cm sandwich tins and put half the mixture in each.

Bake in the preheated oven for approximately 60 minutes.

Leave to cool in the oven.

Whip the double cream. Sandwich the two cake halves together with the cream and half the raspberries.

Using a hand blender, mix together the other half of the raspberries with icing sugar to make the sauce (you decide how sweet you would like it).

When serving, cut a large slice and drizzle with the raspberry sauce.

Dedicated to Prince (the singer, NOT hubby!).

morello cherry bake

serves 8

for the pastry
250g plain flour
85g caster sugar
115g dairy-free margarine
1 teaspoon baking powder
1 large egg

for the filling
2 large eggs
115g dairy-free margarine
115g caster sugar
175g ground almonds
1 teaspoon vanilla essence
2 x 425g tins pitted black cherries, drained

Combine all the ingredients for the pastry and put 140g of it in the freezer. Put the rest in the fridge for 1 hour.

Preheat the oven to 180°C/350°F/gas mark 4.

Take the pastry from the fridge and roll it to fit the bottom of a greased 23cm loose-bottomed tin. (Remove the bottom of the tin, place it on the rolled pastry and draw with a sharp knife around it to get the correct shape.)

Put all the ingredients for the filling in a mixing bowl, apart from the cherries. Blend until you have a smooth paste, then add the cherries. Pour the mixture over the pastry.

Take the frozen pastry out of the freezer and grate it over the top of the cherry mixture. Bake in the preheated oven for 55 minutes.

You will definitely be left wanting More-llo Cherry Bake!

hamantaschen
lulav
couture

a second helping of yiddish, with expression

We are experiencing a new Yiddish expressionism phrase – I mean phase. It is everywhere, from in the newspapers to on TV. Everybody is at it and you don't have to be a Jewish Princess (or even Jewish) to love it.

Yiddish mixed up with the English language is so commonplace that Yiddish has moved on from the *shtetl* (village) and is now out there in the marketplace. I know myself when a Yiddish word pops out of my mouth: I am suddenly gesticulating, waving my arms, waving my hands and raising my eyebrows to the ceiling... After all, Yiddish just isn't Yiddish if it isn't accompanied with a little bit of expressionism.

So in the following pages, I have listed a few Yiddish phrases that I hope will give you a *shtick* (laugh). Don't forget, when you try them out: arms up, hands up, shoulders up, eyebrows up!

*****

My mother will *kvell* (be proud) when she tells all her friends that her daughter is The Jewish Princess.

'Shhh: *nisht* in front of the kinder.' (Not in front of the children.) Mum, what don't you want us to hear?

My husband is a *gantseh macher* (big shot) at work and a *putz* (idiot) at home.

Please don't tell anyone what I said; you know what *yachnas* (gossips) people are.

Have you seen that handbag? It is such a *metsiah* (bargain): only £100, down from £200. Do you think I should buy two?

If you have nothing nice to say, say *nisht.* (Nothing)

My therapist said to tell her what is bothering me. Is she *tsedrayt*? (mad)

My husband is such a *dumkop,* (dumb head). He suggested I should go out to work! I need that like a *loch in kop* (a hole in the head).

It was *bashayrt* (fate) that I went out with my husband. I stalked him for six months.

I *shlepped* (travelled a long way) everywhere to buy these shoes and now my feet are killing me.

So I asked him, 'Does my *tuches* (bottom) look big in these?' He said, 'It depends how far away you stand.' What *chutzpah*! (cheek)

It is such a *krank* (sickness): she can eat whatever she likes and she still looks like a *langer lockshen* (long and thin).

Don't drive me *meshugga* (mad). Even though I am a Jewish Princess, I can't be a *maiven* (expert) at everything.

He is a *meshuggener* (madman). He thinks he really is a *maiven* (expert) at everything.

He made such a *megillah* (song and dance) about it. It was only the credit card bill!

They have so many *chotchkehs* (small ornaments) in that museum, it must take hours to keep that place *shpigelt* (clean).

My husband is such a *shmuck* (the literal meaning is a penis, but this is often used to mean an idiot). My husband is such a *shmerill* (idiot). My husband is such a *shmendrick* (idiot). But I love him!

You remember him? The *nebbish* (nerd), the *nudnik* (a pest), the one that drove me *meshugga* to take me out? He became a brain surgeon.

When you buy heavy items, use your *saychel* (common sense): always have them delivered!

Oh, stop being so *schmaltzy* (over-the-top lovey-dovey); just hand over the ring!

A *shmear* (enough to butter) of cream cheese and a lot of lox (smoked salmon), a slice of lemon and a *bissel* (small amount) of black pepper make the perfect bagel.

His salary had a lot of bagels (zeros) after the 1.

A *bissel* (small amount) more cheesecake, please. Are you sure there are only 100 calories in every bite?

She *shlepped naches* (took a lot of pride) when her *boychik* (little boy) had the lead in the school play. He was a tree.

On *shabbos* (Sabbath) after lunch, *Zaydeh* (Grandfather) usually takes a long *shluff* (sleep).

Always on *simchas* (happy occasions). It is said at happy occasions – and also when someone dies.

The salesman gave such a bad *spiel* (patter) that she advised him, 'Next time you try telephone sales, stay *shtoom* (quiet).'

Are you sure the deal is kosher (legitimate)?

Oh, that *shmai drai* (knick-knack)? It's a Picasso.

Oh, this *shmatta* (piece of cloth)? It's Gucci.

Stop making a *matzo* pudding (a big deal) out of it; I only suggested we go shopping.

Stop *noodging* (irritating) me. I'll go shopping when I am good and ready!

Oy gevalt! The expression to use for when you are shocked – for example when you put on a pound.

Osa (get real) if you think I am going to do the washing up.

The Jewish Princess Feasts & Festivals is full of *chien* (cheeky jokes)!

The recipes in *The Jewish Princess Feasts & Festivals* are a *meichel* for the *beichel* (a gift for the stomach).

Shoyn genug! (That's enough!)

Once a Jewish Princess...

The Jewish Princess gets to the Pearly Gates.

She says, 'Leave the bags outside.
I want to check the rooms before I come in.'

www.thejewishprincess.com